BMW Motorcycle
Buyer's Guide

Mark Zimmerman
and
Brian J. Nelson

MOTORBOOKS

This edition first published in 2003 by Motorbooks International, an imprint of MBI Publishing Company, Galtier Plaza, Suite 200, 380 Jackson Street, St. Paul, MN 55101-3885 USA

The information in this book is true and complete to the best of our knowledge. All recommendations are made without any guarantee on the part of the author or Publisher, who also disclaim any liability incurred in connection with the use of this data or specific details.

We recognize that some words, model names and designations, for example, mentioned herein are the property of the trademark holder. We use them for identification purposes only. This is not an official publication.

Motorbooks International titles are also available at discounts in bulk quantity for industrial or sales-promotional use. For details write to Special Sales Manager at Motorbooks International Wholesalers & Distributors, Galtier Plaza, Suite 200, 380 Jackson Street, St. Paul, MN 55101-3885 USA.

Library of Congress Cataloging-in-Publication Data available
ISBN 0-7603-1164-1

Cover photos by Brian J. Nelson

Edited by Darwin Holmstrom and Kris Palmer
Layout by Stephanie Michaud and Brenda Canales

Printed in China

Contents

Acknowledgements

Nothing happens in a vacuum. Putting this book together without the help of my good friend Phil Cheney would have been impossible. Phil has forgotten more about BMWs than most of us will ever know. Thanks again Phil, I couldn't have done it without you.

Introduction

The title of this book says it all. Over the years, BMW motorcycles have developed a loyal and chauvinistic following. The reason for this is not so much because they were the most exciting bikes on the market—although some of them, both past and present, do have offer surprising performance—but because they're such quietly competent, dependable machines.

In a word, they are "practical"—well built, well designed, and reliable as an anvil. BMWs have always been the choice of the hardened touring rider, the rider who demands a trouble free ride and who appreciates exemplary if sometimes slightly eccentric, engineering. Since the beginning of the marque, BMW ownership has conferred a degree of status matched by few other brands.

BMWs have always marched to a different drummer. Over the years the bikes have managed by turns to be on the cutting edge of technology and as conservative as a minister. (On the cutting edge, BMW was the first to embrace the telescopic fork, and on the conservative side, until 1970 BMWs were for the most part painted black or white, and mostly black.) They also had a well-deserved reputation for oddball designs, many of which featured genuinely good ideas. (Both the Telelever fork and the Earles fork coming quickly to mind.)

When I first entered the world of motorcycles back in the dark ages of the middle 1960s, BMWs were the only real choice if you were a serious, long-distance rider. Guys like John Penton and Danny Liska were known around the world for their long-distance record-setting rides. Penton liked to ride his R69S from New York to LA as quickly as possible, often in less than 48 hours. Liska wasn't much for speed records—he just liked to ride. And his idea of a good ride was to circumnavigate the globe, in both directions!

But I digress. This book is not a history of BMW. Plenty of good ones are out there, and the authors have done a fine job of ferreting out all you need to know about them. Nor is it a buyer's guide aimed at the hardcore collector, although some of the bikes are truly collectible, and many more of them are likely to become so. My feeling is that if you're the guy looking for a 1929 R63, the first of the 750-cc OHV models, then you'll need more information than I can provide here.

My purpose in writing this book is to provide a guide to those BMWs that are the most practical for the buyer who is purchasing a motorcycle to ride. There are plenty of collectibles in here—it'd be a damned short book if I only covered the last five years of production. But the main thrust is toward bikes that are useable, rather than those regarded as strictly collectible.

—Mark Zimmerman

Chapter 1
Buying a Used Motorcycle

Buying a used BMW motorcycle is one of the safest bets in the used bike market. The numbers prove it. A few years ago, the company built its one-millionth bike. In connection with the event, the company managers decided to do a handlebar count to see how many of those bikes were still in use. They were astonished to discover that over half the bikes built since 1923 were still registered and on the road. That statistic alone tells you an awful lot about BMW quality.

WHY BUY A USED BMW?

The longevity described above is a pretty good reason by itself. Over the years, BMW has built a lot of reliable motorcycles, including some very nice models that had short (at least by BMW standards) production runs. Relatively rare models like the early R65, especially 1978–1981 versions, the R80ST, and the R80GS series make fine and long-lived "working bikes." These are practical motorcycles that can be used daily, while still retaining an air of exclusivity. Actually some Beemerphiles would argue that *all* BMWs fall into this category, and who's to say they're wrong?

Along with the rare models, a good range of daily-use bikes—bikes I call "working classics"—is available. A working classic is a classic or vintage motorcycle that in any sense of the word could be considered a collectible. Yet the working classic is also a motorcycle that can be used on a regular basis. Most of the /2 range of machines come under this heading, as do many of the /5 models, as well as later bikes like the R90S, and R100RS.

Another obvious reason for buying a used BMW is pure economics. In most cases you can save a substantial sum by purchasing a used—or in these days of commercial spin, "preowned"—motorcycle. Two quick phone calls made after I'd written the last sentence turned up a very nice 1983 R100RT with 65,000 miles on it for $3,500 negotiable, and a superclean 1996 K1100RS, with 48K on the clock, for $6,295. Both motorcycles were exceptionally clean and needed virtually nothing, and both should easily approach or exceed the 100,000-mile mark without the need for anything more than routine maintenance.

ACQUIRING

It doesn't really matter whether you're a bargain hunter looking for the best possible deal you can find on a good solid K or oilhead, or someone seeking a nice collectible motorcycle that won't let you down on the road. The practical steps used to acquire a solid BMW are the same.

WHAT IS IT THAT YOU REALLY WANT?

Most of us have a pretty good idea of what we're looking for when we set out to buy a motorcycle. But sometimes it's a good idea to articulate our plan anyway. After all, your always having liked the looks of a particular bike doesn't mean it's the best one for your needs. Certainly you don't want to commit to a model you haven't ridden. To be sure you get something you like to ride, look at and try several different models before narrowing your search to a particular one. Do all the things in your test rides that you'll do once you've bought a bike. Do some slow speed puttering, with tight turns. Park it at the curb. Get out on the highway and open it up. Listen to your body as well as the bike. Do you like where your hands and knees and feet are? You can make some adjustments, of course, but maybe there's another model that feels as if it was made for you. Don't part with your money until you've found the model that feels right for you.

WRECKS AND RESTORATION

We won't get too sidetracked on this subject, because it's off-topic for the typical buyer who's ready to ride. Still, your search—particularly if you're shooting for the lowest price you can find—may lead you to bikes in need of significant repair or restoration. Taking a bike from a basket of parts to a glimmering, purring, testament to your skills and dedication can be very satisfying. But you have to have the skill, time, and temperament to see the project through. A bike that needs restoration may cost you a lot more money than a running example of the same bike would, because you'll pay to repair and replace things you otherwise wouldn't bother with to raise everything to the same high quality of performance and finish.

If you know what you're in for, buying a wreck and rebuilding it can save you a ton of money. It's also a great way to dig yourself into a very deep pit. If the damage is mainly cosmetic, and either you have an "in" at the local BMW shop or you feel comfortable doing the repairs on your own, the bike may turn out to be a great deal. On the other hand, assessing all the damage incurred in an accident is a tough job, even for the experienced professional technician. Steering heads get twisted, frame tubes get tweaked, and lots of hidden, subtle, and budget-busting damage may not come to light until you actually try to assemble the bike or, worse, take it for a ride. If you have the experience, the tools, and time to take on a late-model rebuild, by all means go for it. But unless you are a highly experienced mechanic, I'd advise against it, especially if this is your first foray into BMW ownership.

THE PAPER CHASE

The purpose of this book, as I mentioned in the introduction, is to connect the ready-to-ride buyer with a ready-to-ride motorcycle. Yet some of you, once you've gleaned the descriptions and advice here, may wish to tear deeper into the marque and the distinctions of its models. In that case, you may wish to check out more in-depth works on the subject. I haven't read them all, but I can recommend the *Illustrated Buyer's Guide–BMW Motorcycles* by Stefan Knittel and Roland Slabon, as well as *BMW Motorcycles* by Darwin Holmstrom and Brian J. Nelson.

If you get hooked on performance figures, you may also want to seek out contemporary magazine road tests of the bikes you're considering. Generally these can be found through specialty dealers like Motorcycle Days [(410) 665-

6295], or through the publishers themselves—most have some sort of reprint or back issues department. There is also an outfit called Motorcycle Reports [(303) 777-2385] that will put together a comprehensive package of information that includes not only a road test but owners' reports and letters, tuning and accessory articles, and anything else the researchers can find related to your particular bike.

(See Appendix for additional addresses and phone numbers.)

BUYING THE BIKE—DEALERS VERSUS THE PRIVATE SALE

Is it better to buy a used motorcycle privately, or through a licensed motorcycle dealership? Buying privately offers several advantages. You're likely to save a few bucks. You are also more likely to find the bike you're looking for, simply because you'll be able to cover more territory. And let's be realistic, not many /5 or older models are traded in against a new K12—those older bikes are generally sold by word of mouth, at auction, or through the want ads. On the downside, once a private deal is consummated, that's generally it. Most states have little if any legislation controlling private vehicle sales, so if the bike turns out to have major flaws, you may have only a potential lawsuit for a remedy—with no guarantees you'll win.

Buying through a dealership also offers several tangible benefits. Most shops offer some sort of warranty, regardless of the bike's age or mileage. They don't do this because they are altruistic; they do it to protect their good name, and in some cases because it is mandated by state motor vehicle law. If the bike was originally sold by the dealership, the service records will be readily available, and the fact that the previous owner felt good enough about the shop to purchase another bike there also says something commendable. The dealership can also help with insurance, registration, and all of those other pain-in-the-butt details that complicate buying a motorcycle, including arranging financing.

In most circumstances, any used bike sold while the new bike warranty is still in effect, whether it's sold by a dealer or an individual, will be covered in the event of a breakdown that is specified in the factory warranty. If the bike is still under warranty from the factory, the dealer can help facilitate any paperwork. In many states, dealerships are required by law to provide some sort of written warranty, and any problems can be resolved through the state's department of motor vehicles. I have never heard of any state that requires individuals to provide any warranty at all.

If you buy from a reputable dealership, you should also receive a turn-key motorcycle, one that has been serviced, inspected, and safety checked. You also have some legal recourse, should the bike turn out to be a real lemon. The last brings up a side issue: Most of us feel a little intimidated checking out the mechanical condition of a used motorcycle at a dealership. Don't be—if something doesn't feel right, call it to the salesman's attention. By the same token, if he guarantees the engine's condition, and is willing to stand by it in the form of a warranty, don't insist that he do a compression check right in front of you. Actually most of the dealers that I'm acquainted with will allow a used motorcycle to be taken off the premises to be inspected, or let you bring in an outside mechanic if you're truly serious. They don't encourage it, nor do they like it, but under the right circumstances, they will allow it.

On the down side, most used bikes sold through franchised dealers command a premium price. Selections, of course, are limited only to what people trade in or the dealerships obtain at auction. This may present a problem if you're looking for an older bike, although some dealerships do specialize in vintage machines.

THE NUTS AND BOLTS OF USED BIKE BUYING

With over 30 years in the motorcycle industry, mostly in the service end of things, I think it's fair to say that I've probably inspected well over 1,000 used motorcycles. Many of these were traded in on new bikes, but quite a few were for my own use. I think it's also fair to say that I've learned something in the process about inspecting a used bike—and trust me, I haven't been burned in a very long time.

While it's certainly true that BMW has a fundamentally different approach to building motorcycles from most manufacturers, that doesn't mean BMWs are inspected, serviced, or repaired any differently. Buying a used bike isn't rocket science—essentially, every used motorcycle in the world, whether it's a 50-cc moped or a K1200RS, is inspected in the same basic manner. The next section assumes that you are in the market for a bike that is more or less ready to ride, a turnkey bike as such. If the bike in question fails muster and the repairs would push the cost beyond your budget, then my suggestion is that you pass and move on. Remember we're looking for a practical bike here, not a restoration project.

As a rule of thumb the mechanical inspection of any motorcycle can be divided into two broad categories. First is the general overview of the bike. Basically this is your initial impression of the motorcycle: Is the bike as represented? That is, does it fit the picture formed in your mind when you heard a description of the bike? For example, if the seller said it was in good condition, you may expect minor scratches or dings, but would probably be surprised to find a rusty bike that's been lying around for years partly dismantled. Frankly, most sellers are prone to a little exaggeration, and that's part of the fun. But if the owner has clearly overstated the condition of the bike, then it's time to take a walk, or renegotiate the price.

Second, of course, is the bike's actual mechanical condition. Intuitively you may think that if the bike looks good, its mechanical condition must be in keeping with its appearance. This is customarily true, at least to a point; an owner who takes pride in his machine's appearance ordinarily takes at least the same amount of pride in its mechanicals.

However, this isn't always the case, especially when it comes to older bikes—more than a few of which have been "restored" with a coat of paint and some fresh chrome. On the other hand there always seem to be the odd BMW owners who take a perverse pride in owning a bike that looks like dung, yet runs like a Swiss watch. These people care only about function and not form, never washing or polishing the motorcycle, but rigorous in changing the oil, fluids, performing tune-ups, etc. Go figure. While these bikes are cosmetically challenged, they can be well worth buying, especially if you don't mind a few scratches or some sweat equity to bring them up to snuff.

If the bike is as represented, you can take the owner's word for it that the bike truly is mint and in perfect mechanical condition, or you can "vet" the bike, that is check it out yourself. Because a BMW is a refined piece of machinery, a BMW owner typically cares a lot about the bike, even though it's for sale. Therefore, if you inspect the bike yourself, you'll want to do so carefully, respecting the owner's concern.

MECHANICAL INSPECTION

Motorcycles taken as a whole are fairly complex organisms. Yet when broken down into their various subsystems, they become simpler. In that way BMWs are no different from any other motorcycle. The aim in the inspection process is to break the motorcycle down into its subsystems and inspect them. If the subsystem is determined to be good, we'll move on. If it isn't, we'll try to determine which component is at fault, and how its condition will impact the bike as a whole.

For the most part we'll break the bike down into the following subsystems: cosmetics, which includes the overall condition of the bodywork; the engine/transmission and final drive, which is self-explanatory; the electrical system, which includes the charging system, the lights and the battery, starter motor and ignition, plus the instruments; and the running gear/suspension, which is something of a catchall but includes the fork, the frame, swing arm and rear suspension, tires and steering-head bearings.

Let's start with a few general inspection techniques. The germane issues peculiar to individual models will be covered in the appropriate chapters.

COSMETIC EVALUATION

Since first impressions count for so much, that's where we'll start. Regardless of year, the fit and finish of all new BMW motorcycles ranges from very good to excellent. Because the OEM-applied finish is so good, the bikes normally age well. Of course, if you're looking at an older bike, allowances must be made, particularly if the bike is still in the original livery.

Does it look like the owner took decent care of it? A well-cared-for bike should look it. The paint should be waxed, the chrome polished and the bodywork free of large dents or serious damage. You should make some allowances for normal wear and tear, especially on bikes with high mileage. Stone chips, small scratches, and random dings in the sheet metal are the price you pay for actu-

ally riding the bike; besides they add character. But gouges and scrapes in the paint, dents in the sheet metal or cracks in the fiberglass are indicative at best of a careless owner, and at worst of a tip-over or two.

Rusty parts and corrosion of the aluminum bits indicate that the owner was somewhat neglectful, at least with detail items, but it may also mean that the owner spent a lot of time riding in inclement weather. If the rust is limited to a few pieces of hardware, particularly hardware that is tough to keep clean, I wouldn't be too concerned. But if the rust is evident on things like the axles, crash bars, handlebars, and other major pieces, beware; if the cosmetics are important to you, replacement, or repair of bright work can be expensive. Any serious corrosion of the alloy is a problem. While the various aluminum parts can be refurbished, it's time-consuming and labor intensive, and again it's an indication of how the owner treated the bike.

The painted parts on BMWs normally hold up very well. The one exception is some of the metallic colors used during the 1970s. On occasion the metallic paintjobs have been known to fade or bleach. This is by no means common, but it does happen, primarily to bikes left standing for long periods of time in extremely hot or direct sunlight. Bad paint won't impair the bike's performance, but it is expensive to repair, and is a real issue if appearance is important to you. Peeling paint around the battery carrier area is a sure sign that battery acid was spilled. The spill may have resulted from a cracked battery, improperly routed vent hose, or an overcharged battery. As long as there is no structural damage caused by the acid, the problem is strictly cosmetic. If there is severe rusting or pitting, you'll need to decide what kind of repairs are needed and act accordingly.

Take a look at the valve covers, particularly on any of the airhead twins. If the bike was ridden hard, the covers will show it. Some scrapes are normal and don't necessarily mean the bike was dropped or abused.

On some models, particularly /5, /6 and /7s, the brake pedal may also touch down during spirited riding. The kickstand and centerstand will also drag on occasion, and scrapes here only mean the pilot was brave. While you're down there, take a look at the centerstand lever, principally on the 5 through 7 series bikes. Many were broken off from improper use when the bikes were new. Both earlier and later model bikes had better stands, which eliminated that little glitch. K bikes are also known to drag the stands once in a while, so a scrape or two there is of no concern. I once spent the day in the company of a very accomplished rider on a K100RS. He amazed me by dragging the right rear corner of the saddlebag through some of the turns. What amazed me the most was that nothing else on the bike touched down. If you see a ground-off saddlebag corner on a K, and the owner tells you he did it while pushing the envelope, believe him.

The fiberglass on full-fairing bikes should be intact. As a rule, BMW uses very good glass that isn't prone to cracking or spider webbing. Cracks in the fairing are the result of a collision with a hard surface. Take a glance at the mounting brackets as well: If they show signs of having been bent and then straightened, assume the bike was dropped, and dropped fairly hard. From the seat, the fairing should have a uniform fit. The gaps on either side of the tank should be about equal. If the fairing is noticeably offset, it's better than even money that it took a serious shove to move it that way.

The seat cover should be free from rips and tears; any seat emblems should be positioned symmetrically. If the emblems are off-center, it means that the cover has been replaced by someone who didn't take much pride in his work. From 1969 to 1980 the /5, /6 and /7 seats have a trim strip along the lower edges; depending on the year and model, these may be either tin or plastic. The plastic ones do have a tendency to craze over or even crack; this is normal, though not very desirable.

Overall, the bike should look as if it was well taken care of, at the very least commensurate with its asking price.

THE ELECTRICS

Historically, BMW electrics are given high marks for reliability. The older models used a 6-volt DC generator to charge the battery and power the lights, and either a magneto to generate the sparks (twins) or a battery and DC coil (singles). Starting with the /5 series, the Bosch magneto was exchanged for a DC ignition system and 12-volt alternator. Be aware that a few pre-1970 bikes, particularly /2 models, have been converted over to 12-volt electrics. Also, a few /2s (mainly police bikes) came from the factory with 12-volt charging systems. In the main, this is a worthwhile conversion, so long as it was properly done.

It's tough to evaluate the condition of the electrics with a cursory inspection. The wiring harness, at least where it is visible, should be in good repair. Older bikes may have a wrap or two of electrical tape at points where the harness flexes. Take a look at the harness where it makes the bend around or under the steering stem. Some chaffing here is normal; better a wrap of tape than an exposed wire loom. But big gobs of tape wrapped around a section of harness indicate that a repair was made at some point. By the way, it's been my experience that the more tape, the less professional the repair.

The battery terminals should be clean and tight, and the battery water should be set to the correct level. It goes without saying that all the lights and the horn should work. Switches, particularly on an older bike, are an occasional source of trouble. Problems are usually brought about by overzealous washing—many times they can be repaired with nothing more than a few shots of WD-40.

With the exception of the R50/5, all post-1969 models have electric starters. These should engage smoothly and spin the engine over quickly. The /5 models have undersized batteries, so if you're looking at a bike that hasn't been run in awhile or you're looking at the bike during a cold spell, the starter may be reluctant to spin the motor over. My advice is to use the kick-starter a few times to free up the engine before trying to use the electric starter.

Once the bike is running, the charge indicator light should go out on all models at any engine speed above a fast idle. If it doesn't, charging problems are present or fast approaching. Depending on the model, these can range from the easy and inexpensive—worn brushes in the generator or alternator—to very expensive—perhaps a burnt out generator, alternator, or diode board. If the charge light doesn't come on when the ignition is switched on, first check that the bulb isn't burnt out. If the bulb is good and the light doesn't come on with the switch, then it's a safe bet that the alternator rotor is kaput.

On older models, magneto trouble can cause everything from hard starting to a high-speed miss. The problem that you are most likely to encounter is that magneto coils can act up when they get hot; a brief road test may not allow a suspect coil to get hot enough to show a problem. Normally if the bike starts easily and runs well, the magneto is probably fine. I hate to be so vague but there is really no way to assess the mag's condition with any accuracy. If you're looking at a magneto-equipped motorcycle, it throws a good healthy spark, and the bike runs well, assume that the magneto is probably good. If the bike won't start and there is no spark, it doesn't necessarily mean that the mag is bad, but it does mean you'll need to investigate a bit deeper.

I must confess that I don't have a lot of practical, hands-on experience with late-model BMW electrics. Obviously the electronics are very sophisticated, what with fuel injection and ABS, not to mention heated grips and seats, stereos, and so forth. I do know that for the most part, the latest generation electrics are very reliable but are difficult to troubleshoot, especially without the proper training and diagnostic tools. My advice is to seek the opinion of a qualified BMW mechanic should any questions arise. If a late-model bike does display any type of electrical faults I'd say pass, unless the seller is willing to have the bike checked out and repaired before you exchange any money.

The instruments should work smoothly; they are expensive to repair and even more costly to replace. The one exception is the cable-driven tachometer fitted to the /5 and /6 models. These tend to wander a bit, and while I've seen them run the gamut from flicker to fluctuate, I've yet to see one that was rock steady. Some early K bikes also had instrument cluster problems. Since most of these were replaced under warranty when the bikes were new, bad ones are somewhat rare. But they are out there. K bikes may also have a fogging problem. This isn't all that serious an issue, and updated lenses and seals are available to correct it.

FLASHING ABS LIGHTS/ABS INACTIVE

This is a fairly common problem with bikes that have sat for a while. You may run into a situation in which either the ABS lights flash or the ABS refuses to run through the self-check and won't function. The owner may seem genuinely surprised at this and swear it's never happened before. If the bike has been sitting for any length of time believe him. If battery voltage is low, the ABS disengages and the lights will flash. Usually a quick battery charge is all that's needed to put things right; in a worst case you may need to replace the battery. Be aware that any serious ABS problem can be expensive to put right. If the ABS light stays on, it indicates a problem that will have to be dealt with by an authorized BMW dealer. I'd probably pass on any bike with an ABS malfunction. As an alternative, provided the owner is agreeable, have the bike checked out by the local BMW shop before proceeding; at least that way you'll know what you're up against, and you and the seller can negotiate accordingly.

ACCESSORY ITEMS

Over the years BMW has seen fit to equip its bikes with everything from spotlights to heated seats and CD players. Of course any factory-installed electrical options should work. If not, the repair cost should be figured into the price of the bike. Nonworking electrical accessories are a real minefield, primarily because the components are so expensive. It's one thing if a fog light isn't working, quite another if the cruise control fitted to a K1200 gives up the ghost. Not everyone wants or needs all the whistles and bells. If you can live without a particular option, more power to you, and you may be able to realize quite a savings.

Owner-installed options are another matter. If you don't like them, they are typically easy to remove. If you decide to keep them, make certain that they are properly installed and wired correctly. Wiring should be protected with either tape or an external shield, and the connections should be properly crimped or, better yet, soldered. The device itself should be fused and, if required, a relay used to power the circuit.

ENGINES, TRANSMISSIONS, AND FINAL DRIVES ENGINES

As a rule, all BMW engines should be mechanically quiet. The older twins in particular were extremely quiet, and any mechanical clatter can be construed as a bad omen. The big problem with the /2 and earlier models is that they had no real oil filtration system. Slinger rings were mounted to the end of the crankshaft. As oil was pumped through the crankshaft, centrifugal force caused the heavy dirt particles to be thrown outward, where they would lodge in the slinger rings. The problem is that if sludge builds up in the rings it overflows into the big end bearings, resulting in some very serious (and expensive) damage.

Opinions vary on the life expectancy of the slinger rings, although modern oils have done a lot to prolong their life. The factory used to recommend cleaning them out every 30,000 miles or so. But many, many riders doubled and tripled that mileage without any problem. Lamentably, short of dismantling the engine and having a look at the crankshaft, there is no way of knowing how much sludge is packed into the rings. You may have 50,000 miles of life left, or 5. This is one instance when you'll need to trust the owner. If he has changed the oil regularly and the bike appears to be well kept, chances are the bottom end will be fine. If the bike is rough-and-tumble, consider it a rolling time bomb.

With the introduction of the /5 line in 1969, plain bearing crankshafts became the norm. Accordingly, modern high-pressure lubrication systems, complete with replaceable filters, were adapted. These bottom ends are bulletproof; if one is making noise, pass—it's a sure sign of owner abuse, and an impending disaster.

Some twin cylinder top ends can be a little noisy. The airhead twins built from 1969 to 1993 use the cylinder hold-down studs to locate the rocker arms. During normal running, end play can develop between the pillow blocks that locate the rocker arms and the rockers themselves. The rocker arm-to-pillow block clearance can and should be adjusted every time the valves are adjusted, provided of course that the owner is aware of it. Many second, third, and fourth owners aren't; they just think the top ends rattle a little and let it go.

The /5 rocker arms used a plain bushing that tended to wear and was a bit noisy in operation. Starting with the /6, needle bearings replaced the bushings. Occasionally one of these bearings will break up. Normally the valve will start to clatter before any real damage is done. The repair is simple— replace the bad bearing, adjust the valve and get back on the road.

OILHEADS

As of this writing, the oil engines have certainly lived up to or maybe exceeded expectations. They have proven to be mechanically trouble free. High-mileage motors should be checked as you would any other engine—if the mill is quiet, doesn't smoke or leak, and runs well, you can be reasonably assured that the powerplant is sound.

K BIKES

K75 Three-cylinder engines are just about bulletproof, and I'm unaware of any chronic problems. I have heard of a few (actually a very few) four-cylinder engines that wore out their bores at relatively low mileages. These seem to be isolated and somewhat random incidents—some of the machines that were affected were extremely well maintained, and some appeared to have led very difficult lives. One thing is for sure though, the repair is an expensive proposition. Because the K cylinders are cast in unit with the block and are plated, you can't just rebore the cylinders and fit oversize pistons. A replacement short block must be installed, and these get very expensive, as does the labor to install it. Heavy smoking after the bike has been ridden for a bit is one indication that the cylinders are shot, as is poor overall performance. The right way to assess the condition of the bore is with a leak-down test. Since most of us don't own a leak-down tester, this is a job left to a pro. If a bike that interests you displays any evidence of a worn bore, I'd suggest that you have a pro, particularly one with lots of K bike experience, check the bike out—after all, there are other things that can cause the same symptoms. If the owner balks at this suggestion, I'd pass on the bike, or be prepared to spend a big chunk of cash repairing it, should it require a fresh top end.

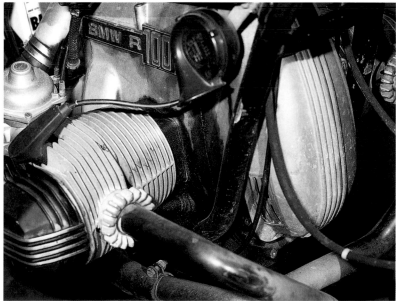

SINGLES

The older pushrod singles are as straightforward as a Briggs and Stratton engine. Check them out as you would any other pushrod single. If they run well, don't smoke and are quiet, chances are they are fine. Of course they also use slinger ring oil "filters" and are subject to the problems described above if neglected. But by and large they are solid engines. If they have any chronic flaws, it's the charging system, which has always been a bit spotty. Charging system parts are also expensive and may be scarce.

Late singles are very nice motors. The ones built by Aprillia under contract are first rate, and the late BMW-built models are even better.

BMW IDIOSYNCRASIES

Kickstand Smoke

BMWs have a singular peculiarity in the relationship between the cylinder placement and the kickstand. When the kickstand is deployed, the left cylinder of the twin-cylinder models and the entire cylinder bank of the K models lies downhill. This causes oil to run down the cylinder wall, creep past the ring end gaps and enter the combustion chamber. On start-up the affected cylinder(s) will smoke like a chimney. Under normal conditions the smoke vanishes after a few minutes and all is well. Experienced BMW owners rarely park their bikes on the kickstand for more than a few minutes at a time. If the bike you're checking out is parked on the stand, chances are good that the owner doesn't have a lot of experience with BMW, is incredibly lazy, or just doesn't give a hoot. All good reasons to offer him a low-ball price and ride off into the sunset as soon as the smoking stops.

Crankcase Blow-By

Crankcase blow-by or, more correctly, crankcase pressurization, is a problem commonly associated with the airhead twins built from 1970 on. The outward symptoms are oil leaks, particularly from the rear main seal, and lots of oil pumping out of the crankcase breather. BMW originally assumed that the problem lay with the rear main seal and redesigned the seal accordingly. At the same time there were also some concerns with the breather system, and that was modified as well. But the bikes kept leaking. Owners began to complain of high oil consumption, particularly on the 900- and 1,000-cc motors. Eventually the problem was traced to what we might consider overprotective owners.

Most owners were reluctant to really thrash their new

and, by the standards of the day, expensive motorcycles. They tended to break in the bikes very gently. Riders who really put the coal to their bikes had few if any problems. BMW soon realized that the break-in procedure was overly restrictive—new engines simply weren't being broken in at all, let alone properly. Once the rings glazed over, combustion gases leaked past them, and pressurized the crankcase faster than they could be vented through the breather. Having two large pistons reach bottom dead center at the same time didn't help matters. The solution was simple: bikes that had problems were torn down, the cylinders deglazed (and allowed to acquire a very slight patina of rust) and new rings installed dry, that is without any lubricating oil, which was contrary to the practice of the day; only the piston skirt got a small smear of oil. The engine was then assembled. On the initial start-up the engine was held at 3,000 rpm until it stopped smoking; it was then taken for a brisk ride. The modified break-in procedure stopped 99 percent of the problems, and the same techniques are still used today.

Occasionally you'll find a restored or rebuilt airhead exhibiting all the classic signs of a pressurized crankcase. The cause can usually be traced directly to an inexperienced rebuilder, or to an overly gentle rider. The solution is simple: take the bike for the kind of ride it was meant for. If the engine has been run less than 1,000 miles, my suggestion would be to run the bike like it was meant to be run for 500 miles and see if the problems subside. If they don't, it's time for a set of rings and a proper break-in.

Valve Recession

Shortly after the feds mandated the removal of lead

from all gasoline, BMW decided to change the exhaust valve seat material used in the R model engines. While its sentiments were in the right place, the execution was lacking. The new material was unsuited for use as a valve seat, as it had poor heat transfer characteristics. Most of the R models built between 1980 and 1984, particularly the R100s, suffer from valve seat recession. (This is one reason the R100 was dropped from the U.S. market from 1984 to 1988, while the less-stressed R80 was still imported.) Because the valve seats are so soft, and without lead to cushion the valve's closure, the valves sink or recede into them.

As valve clearance is lost, performance starts to drop off. Early signs of trouble include hard starting and a poor idle. You can forestall the problem, but at some point updated seats, introduced in 1988, should be installed. Bikes built from 1970 to 1979 are not as prone to valve-seat recession as the 1980–1984 models, but it is a possibility. When contemplating the purchase of any of the /5 through /7 twins, pay close attention to the idle. If the bike won't idle properly it may be due for new seats. If the bike is a 1980–1984 model, find out if the seats have, in fact, been replaced. Since most of the bikes in question have already been repaired, or are likely candidates for a valve job anyway, the situation is more of a nuisance than a real problem. Furthermore, the repair is straightforward and reasonably cheap, and can be performed by any competent shop. It also cures the problem for good, so don't let it keep you from buying an otherwise good motorcycle.

Transmissions—Lurching and Input Splines, All Models

Starting with the /5 models, BMWs sometimes developed some odd transmission behavior. Riders would occasionally complain that the clutch seemed to engage too quickly. This was soon found to involve two problems. The more minor problem was caused by a dry input shaft spline. The clutch disc would hang up on the dry, rusty spline for an instant before engaging the pressure plate and cause the bike to lurch forward. The repair was simple: owners were advised to remove the transmission periodically and lubricate the spline. The second problem was a little more severe: some transmissions had been improperly shimmed at the factory. As the transmissions wore with normal use, the input shaft endplay increased to an unacceptable level. When the clutch was let out, the shaft would move forward in the case, allowing the clutch to engage too quickly.

The symptoms are easy to spot. Afflicted bikes will have clutches that are difficult to engage smoothly. The bikes will leap forward as the clutch is let out. The cure is easy enough: first try lubricating the input shaft splines with a molybdenum-type lube. If that doesn't do it, you'll probably have to reshim the transmission input shaft—a job best left to the dealer.

In a worst case scenario, you may find that the clutch disc and/or the input shaft splines have worn thin. If so, it's better to replace the worn parts now, rather than have them fail on the road.

Rear Wheel Splines / Drive Shaft Problems

ALL BMWs need to have their rear wheel hub drive splines periodically greased with a molybdenum-type lubricant. If this small but crucial maintenance task is overlooked, the splines can fail and forward motion, at least under engine power, becomes a bit of a problem. On-the-ball mechanics and do-it-yourselfers apply antiseize or some like compound every time the wheel is off. Short of removing the wheel, this is one of those things that can be difficult to check, but it never hurts to ask the owner if the splines have been greased lately.

Checking Rear Wheel Splines

Hand in hand with worn transmission input splines are worn rear wheel splines. BMW rear wheels are driven by a set of fine splines. The splines are riveted to the rear wheel and engage a matching set of splines that are part of the ring gear. If the splines are left dry they can wear prematurely. The repair is a bit involved and can be expensive. The application of an antiseize compound to the splines prevents damage from occurring, and some sort of lubricant, preferably a molybdenum-type paste, should be applied any time the wheel is off the bike. To check the splines, place the bike in gear (with the engine off) and try to move the wheel back and forth. If the wheel seems to have excess movement (obviously this is a very subjective test), pull the rear wheel and visually inspect the splines; if they appear to be worn to any great degree, have a BMW technician examine the wheel and final drive before any money changes hands.

DRIVE LINE PROBLEMS

Running Gear: Forks, Frames, Steering Head Bearings, Swing Arms and Rear Suspension, Tires, Wheels, and Brakes

Until the introduction of the "oilheads" in 1993, BMW running gear, with the exception of the Earles fork, was fairly conventional. After 1993 things changed. You'll have to decide for yourself if it was for the better.

Conventional Forks

All of the conventional, which is to say telescopic, forks are checked in the same manner. The fork arms should appear to be in the same plane when viewed from the side. Look for signs of oil leaking. If the bike has rubber gaiters, grasp the gaiter and rub it against the fork tube. If the gaiter feels sticky against the tube and seems to resist movement, it means the fork seals are in good shape. If the gaiter slides easily, it often means the forks seals are weeping so that fork oil is lubricating the rubber. This test is a subjective one and may be misleading, but if the left side slides freely while the right binds, you can be reasonably certain that fork seals will need replacing in the near future.

With the bike on the wheels, hold the front brake on and pump the fork up and down a few times. The fork should move freely in both directions, and no odd squeaks, rattles, or moans should be heard, at least not coming from the fork arms. A clunking sound or movement at the steering head is a bad sign, as it indicates loose steering head bearings.

Place the bike on its centerstand, with the front wheel clear of the ground. A helper can weight the rear of the bike, although most BMWs will balance with either wheel in the air. Grasp the lower fork legs slightly above the axle and try to push the legs forward and backward. If you feel any play or see movement at the fork clamp, the steering head bearings are loose. Loose steering head bearings may just need to be adjusted; however, it's even money that the loose steering head bearings are dented, meaning they'll have to be replaced. This isn't an enormous undertaking but it will cost several hundred dollars if you elect to have a shop do it.

While you're down there, grasp the front wheel at right angles to the fork and try to rock it side to side. If play is noticeable, the wheel bearing will need shimming or replacement.

Slowly spin the wheel: It should turn freely and smoothly. If it grabs, makes noise, or feels rough you'd better plan on at least cleaning and repacking the wheel bearings, or more likely replacing them.

Once you're back on your feet, with the front wheel still clear of the pavement, turn the handlebars from side to side (turn the steering damper off, if the bike has one). The fork should turn smoothly from side to side. If it resists turning or feels as if it drops into a detent, the steering head bearings have dented. In any case, if you suspect worn steering head bearings, the bearings will require removal, inspection and most likely replacement before the bike can be safely ridden.

Earles Forks

While the Earles-forked models may look a lot different from the telescopic-forked bikes, the wheel and steering head bearings are checked in the same manner. Check the shocks for oil leaks: if oil is visible on the shock, the only solution is replacement. Check the pivot point at the rear of the fork swing arm. Grasp it and give it a good pull. There shouldn't be any play—if there is, check the pivot bolts and bearings. Normal play can be adjusted out, and replacement is seldom required*. By the way, for solo use, the pivot bolts should be placed in the hole closest to the engine (the rear holes). For sidecar use, the pivot is placed in the mounting holes closest to the front wheel (the forward holes)—this reduces trail, making the bike easier to steer when a sidecar is mounted. Every once in a while, I'll run across a solo bike with the pivot point in the sidecar position. This makes for interesting handling, to say the least.

* Oddly, pre-1964 model Earles forks had no grease fittings on the front swing arm. Accordingly water could find its way in and rust the bearings. If the bike is pre-1964 and there are no grease fittings retrofitted to the front swing arm, pay close attention to the swing arm action and double check any play.

Telelevers

The Telelever front end, used on the oilhead twins, is quite difficult to check in the traditional manner. Make sure the shock absorber isn't leaking and that the fork moves smoothly. If the front end feels odd during the road test, you'll need to dismantle the fork to find the cause—actually, if the fork gives any cause for concern, it might be best to have your favorite BMW shop take a look at it.

Frames

The BMW frames applicable to the models covered in this guide come in four varieties. Early frames cover the years from 1950 to 1969. They are incredibly robust and can take a real beating. Frames of the middle years cover the airhead twins from 1969 to 1995. These aren't quite as robust and in fact seem a bit spindly at times, but are actually pretty decent. The third style is the oilhead "nonframes." And finally, the fourth variety is the K bikes' tube frame.

The early frames are massive, and while they can be damaged, terminal damage is rare. Essentially you'll want to check the frame gussets for cracks, particularly around the steering head, look for dents in the frame rails, and check around the battery box for signs of corrosion.

The slash 5, 6 and 7 frames have some minor problems. Slash five subframes were drilled to accommodate the taillight wiring. The subframes would often crack at the holes. Most of these were simply welded up, and probably more than a few were replaced with the updated, solid subframe fitted from 1974 on. Another trouble spot is the centerstand mount. The centerstand mounting bolts tend to loosen and strip, requiring a Helicoil or other form of repair. Rough treatment can also cause severe wear to occur to the centerstand stops. In such cases, deploying the stand still leaves both wheels firmly planted on the ground. Repairs

are straightforward but it's another thing to consider when you negotiate price. As an aside, there were aftermarket stands offered that allowed both wheels to remain on the ground. These stands, made by the Reynolds company, have a distinctive appearance and are unlike a factory stand.

After the introduction of the RS in 1976 the welded steering stop, which is mounted to the center of the steering head, was drilled to allow the fitting of a 6-millimeter bolt. The bolt was intended to limit the turning radius of the front fork so the RS bars wouldn't foul the tank. On all other models, the drilled hole simply reduced the strength of the stop. In the event of a relatively minor accident, the fork could shear the drilled stop clean off the steering head. This is definitely an area that should be checked. If the stop appears to have been damaged and repaired, find out what happened. This type of stop is also used on the K bikes.

K bike frames are lightweight and very strong. Since most of the frame resides under the fuel tank and seat, there isn't much that can happen to one short of a catastrophic prang. Again, check around the steering head for any signs of damage. Flaking paint often indicates a crack or inexpertly repaired damage, but unless the bike has been in a horrendous crash, it's unlikely that a K will have any frame problems.

Oilheads

Being somewhat unconventional, the oilheads have no true frame. Everything bolts (eventually) to the engine and transmission. A subframe does hold the seat and lights on. This is either broken or bent, or it isn't. Remove the seat and take a look. I have heard of some oilheads on which the swing arm pivot bolt threads have stripped out of the transmission. This is a potentially serious problem: If any play is felt at the pivot, you'll want to investigate what's going on before proceeding much further.

Swing Arms / Rear Suspensions

Conventional swing arms with twin shocks were used on all models except the GS and the K bikes up to 1984. In that year, the single-sided swing arm and single damper unit, much the same as that used on the GS, was adopted for general use. The shock was mounted without linkage, so checking the rear suspension is straightforward. No leaks should be apparent at the shock itself, and the swing arm pivot shouldn't have any play in it. When viewed from the rear, the wheel should be centered in the swing arm, and

SHOCKING

Aftermarket suspension is one of the more common owner-made modifications. While many owners do try and keep their bikes "catalog original," just as many, particularly those who ride their bikes regularly, upgrade the original suspension. In most cases the aftermarket suspension is installed after the OEM stuff has gone to that big boneyard in the sky, or perhaps to try to improve handling. Airheads are most often in need of shock therapy, if only for age-related reasons. Up front you'll usually find a spring kit, perhaps with modified damping rods. In the rear you'll often encounter replacement rear shocks, usually made by Progressive, Works Performance, Hagon, or perhaps Koni.

As a rule, BMW suspension tends to be a little on the soft side, particularly after a few decades of hard use, and most upgrades are worthwhile. Oilhead bikes, particularly the sport models, are regularly fitted with Ohlins, White Power, or even Penske dampers. These shocks work exceptionally well, and are worth every penny. Pre-1970s models may be fitted with anything from Koni to Boge. As in the case of the airheads, these bikes generally get a new set of boingers because the old ones are plain worn out.

Don't be put off by upgraded replacement suspension—by and large, it's a good thing. If the owner still has the original stuff on the shelf, even better; they'll be useful if you ever decide to show the bike.

both arms should be parallel. Check the rear wheel bearing exactly as you would the front. Check swing arms for play by grasping them close to pivot and trying to move them from side to side. Remember that the swing arm pivots are adjustable, and in most cases a slight bit of play is no cause for concern.

The oilhead bikes, except the Cruisers, use the Paralever suspension system. Check these as you would a Monolever. The swing arm shouldn't have any side-to-side play to it. The shock should be leak free and able to move smoothly through its stroke.

WHEELS AND TIRES

This is short and sweet. Check the wheel bearings by grasping the rim top and bottom, positioning yourself at right angles to the axle, and trying to rock the wheel (at 90 degrees to the axle). If you feel play, the bearing will require adjustment or replacement. Inspect the rims for dings and dents. Early mag wheels were notoriously soft. They are also expensive to replace, and straightening a dented one really isn't an option. Aluminum rims tend to deform somewhat over time. If the rim isn't 100 percent true, it's not a real big deal, but if it looks like a stop sign, consider the price of a

replacement. Give the rim a spin. It should turn smoothly and should be relatively true.

Loose spokes have never been a big issue with BMWs. Even after lots of hard miles the large-gauge, straight-pull spokes used to construct BMW wire wheels seem to hold their tension better than most others. If you'd like, give each one a tap with a screwdriver blade or something. A clear ring means they're nice and snug, but if the wheel looks true, I'll bet the spokes are properly tensioned. On the other hand, any broken or missing spokes indicate hard use, and an overall lack of concern by the owner. The exceptions to the rule are the early R90/6 models. The rims on this bike had a tendency to crack around the spoke holes. I'd imagine most of these rims have been replaced by now, but you never know.

Tires should have at least 50 percent of their tread left. If they don't, consider them candidates for replacement. Check the sidewalls for dry rot, cracks, and weather checking.

In general, BMWs don't suffer from the wheel alignment problems common to chain-driven bikes. However, if the wheels are drastically out of line, it may mean a bent frame, fork, or swing arm. Checking the wheel alignment is somewhat tedious. If the bike handles well during the road test, assume that the wheels are in alignment; if the bike handles poorly or does anything weird while you're riding it, you'll have to decide whether that particular bike is worth further investigation.

BRAKES

Drum brakes should work smoothly and stop the bike without shuddering. The front cable-operated brake in particular is prone to adjustment problems. If you feel anything unusual, watch the actuating levers on the front backing plate while someone pulls the lever. Both arms should move together; if they don't, the brake cams will need adjusting. Obviously the cable itself should be in good condition. Check the cable and foot brake rod—is there any adjustment left? Or has the adjusting screw been wound up tight, indicating worn shoes? One obscure problem that crops up every so often is improper installation of the front brake springs during shoe replacement. The thicker return spring should always be installed on the front brake arm; if it isn't, the actuating arms will not pull in unison, and this can create all sorts of odd brake behavior.

Starting with the slash 6 models in 1974, BMW installed a front disc brake on everything except the R60. R90S and 100RS models got two discs; everything else made do with one. BMW saw fit to mount the master cylinder under the fuel tank on these models. It wasn't really a bad idea. Under the tank, the master cylinder was protected from the elements, and it made for a clean-looking handlebar. Its location does make the master cylinder hard to inspect, though. Since I doubt if many owners will let you remove the fuel tank just to inspect the condition of the master cylinder, you'll have to take it on faith that the fluid is in good condition. Starting with the 1979 models, the master cylinder was relocated to the handlebar, which if nothing else made checking the fluid a lot easier.

Check both the clarity and level of the brake fluid. It should be relatively clear and set to the correct level. All visible brake hoses should be in good shape, that is, free of cracks, kinks and leaks. In fact, any leak from any portion of the brake system is a cause for concern. Check the brake pads themselves—normally there is a window cut in the brake pad material to allow you to check the pad wear. Aftermarket pads may have a different type of indicator; nonetheless, it will be fairly obvious and should give a clear indication as to pad life.

The brake rotors should be relatively smooth. Some ridges and grooves are inevitable, notably on older machines, but they should be neither too deep nor too numerous. As with cable-operated units, the brakes should move smoothly and shouldn't drag.

THE ROAD TEST

This is everyone's favorite part—everyone but the owner. Few of us look forward to letting someone ride our motorcycles. Bear in mind that you are assessing the bike with the idea of purchasing it, not trying to qualify for a national road-race. Treat the seller and his bike with exactly the same courtesy that you would expect were positions reversed.

Your first priority should be the engine. Start the bike and let it warm up. The bike should start easily and, unless it was parked on the kickstand, there should be no dark smoke pumping out the exhaust. Some white vapor is acceptable, particularly if the ambient temperature is cool. As the bike warms up it should settle down to a smooth, steady idle. Ragged idles, particularly on 1970 to 1984 twins, indicate potential valve seat problems.

The engine should be mechanically quiet. If the thing sounds like a threshing machine, thank the owner for his

time and head home. As the engine warms up, watch the indicator lights. Obviously different models will have different combinations of lights and gauges, but as a rule, the oil pressure light, assuming one is fitted, should go out and stay out as soon as the engine is started. Depending on the idle speed, the charge indicator should go out, or indicate that the system is charging at any speed above a high idle.

While you're waiting, familiarize yourself with the controls. It's also a good idea to tug on the various levers, especially the brakes, to make sure that they actually are connected to something. As you twist the throttle pay attention to the way the engine responds: pick up should be smooth and predicable. Hiccups, bogs, and uneven response all indicate the need for some carburetion work.

Any airhead BMW should have the clutch freeplay set at something around 3 millimeters (1/8 inch). Slightly more or less is permissible, but clutches with too little freeplay will slip, while excess freeplay makes for hard shifting. Oilheads should have 12 millimeters of freeplay at the gearbox lever and 7 millimeters of freeplay at the handlebar.

The gearbox should engage first gear easily. Clutch take-up should be progressive. If the clutch action seems sudden, the bike perhaps leaping forward as you let the clutch out, it may mean that the transmission-input shaft requires lubrication. Of course it may also mean that the tranny needs shimming or that several expensive parts need to be replaced.

All clutches are controlled by engine speed. However BMW motorcycles (and Moto Guzzi) have their clutches mounted directly to the crankshaft. They turn at the exact same rpm as the engine—hence they are called "engine speed clutches." All other motorcycles have their clutches driven through a reduction gear, so they spin at something less than crankshaft speed. Due to their engine-speed clutches BMWs have a tendency to be slow and clunky shifters. With practice BMW pilots learn to shift their bikes as well as any other but if this is your first ride on a BMW expect a few clunks from the gearbox. This is particularly true of the old four-speed models—less so with modern bikes. All of the F650 models should shift like any other modern bike. While shifting of many older BMWs might best be described as "agricultural," they should all engage the gears cleanly. Missed shifts, or worse, transmissions that jump out of gear, indicate serious problems.

The motorcycle should accelerate briskly; even the older models should be able to keep up with the normal flow of traffic. That being said, most of the 500-cc bikes, and all of the pushrod singles, accelerate at a leisurely pace. Don't expect superbike acceleration when you crack the throttle on an R27. The bikes should remain mechanically quiet, even at high rpm.

Pop the bike into high gear and accelerate from about 45 miles per hour to 65 or so. Engine rpm should rise in proportion to road speed. A rapid increase in rpm without a proportionate increase in motorcycle velocity means the clutch is slipping. If the clutch slips it's going to need replacement. During the same test the engine should respond smoothly and predictably. If it starts wheezing and coughing like a three-pack-a-day smoker, it may need anything from a tune-up to a top end.

At partial throttle, the bike should run smoothly with no tendency to surge or miss—the exception possibly being low mileage fuel-injected twins. All of those that I've ridden have had a noticeable lean surge at low speed. This is normal and seems to diminish with mileage.

As the throttle is opened, the bike should respond instantly, although the rate of forward progress will vary according to model. At stops, the engine should settle down to a smooth and consistent idle. If an airhead hunts and pecks, the valve seats and valves need attention. On other bikes, particularly the fuel-injected ones, an uneven idle most likely means it's time for a major engine service. At no time should smoke be visible from the exhaust. A bike that smokes constantly needs some serious attention. One that smokes primarily when you let off the throttle is likely in need of valve guides.

Handling is a very subjective thing and an area where problems are often difficult to assess. In general the bike should track straightly and predictably when pointed down the road. It should go around corners without any drama and remain stable at any normal road speed. The suspension should be firm, but compliant. If the fork dives excessively during braking, a common fault on /5-7 models, a fork overhaul may be on the menu. These aren't particularly expensive and make for a better bike. Bottoming at the rear, particularly on twin-shock models, means it's time for new suspenders—again, on post-1970 airheads this is a relatively cheap upgrade. On /2 models and mono-shock bikes it gets a bit dearer.

If the bike tends to shake its head when decelerating, particularly in the 45- to 30-mile per hour range, a steering head bearing adjustment, or replacement, should put things right. Other likely culprits are mismatched tire tread patterns or worn tires.

BMWs are not the best-handling motorcycles in the world, but they are not bad. Late model oilheads are in fact pretty good handling machines. If the bike seems to resist turning, tries to stand up in the middle of a turn, or shimmies and shakes from pillar to post, something is wrong and needs investigating.

The brakes should work smoothly and the action should be predictable. If the brakes shudder it usually means the drum is out of round or the disc is warped, whatever the case may be. Front drum brake "judder" may also be caused by improper adjustment, loose steering head bearings and binding brake cables. A mushy feel at the front disc can come from air in the hydraulic system or worn-out brake hoses.

If the bike is ABS equipped, any faults or concerns should be taken up with an authorized service center. These are tricky systems to bleed and maintain, and I wouldn't take ABS problems lightly.

Upon your return, let the bike idle for a minute or two while you search for any oil or coolant leaks; here too, the idle should be consistent.

If everything is to your satisfaction, it's time to make a deal. If it isn't, smile, tell the owner in a polite way that some items need attention, and ask politely if he is willing to lower the price. If anything seems really wrong, thank him and move on to the next bike.

NEGOTIATING THE DEAL

If you decide this is the bike for you, it's time to make a deal. There are all sorts of tricks that chronic used bike buyers employ. In my opinion, most of them are worthless. One guy I know pretends only to have a limited amount of money; he lets a confederate hold a few bucks and then makes a big show of "borrowing" the extra money should the seller remain hard-nosed about the price. Another guy I know likes to catalog everything that's wrong with the bike. I guess his theory is that the owner will become depressed and lower the price accordingly. In my experience, the sellers don't care where you get the money, so long as you get it, and tend to resent nitpicking. This isn't to say that every bike's worth the asking price, but we're assuming here that both bike and price meet your expectations.

So here is my advice. First, decide what you're prepared to pay for a motorcycle and shop accordingly. There is no sense in looking at a fully restored and premium-priced R90S if you can only afford a moderately priced R75/6. Second, be realistic in your assessment of the motorcycle: If the bike needs a major overhaul don't kid yourself into thinking you can do it on the cheap—trust me, you'll be disappointed. Conversely, don't insist that a bike being sold at a reasonable price be catalog perfect; while you may find the odd exception, most bikes aren't. Lastly, be honest with yourself and the seller. There is little point in beating someone's motorcycle up in the hope that he will lower the price.

PRICING

Knowing what to pay for a particular motorcycle is always tough. Is the asking price realistic? Is it low, high, or just right? To help determine trade-in values, motorcycle dealers use something called a "Blue Book." The Blue Book(s) (there are more than one) give the dealer an average trade-in value and average retail price for a motorcycle in good to excellent condition. These prices are obtained by periodically surveying dealers and averaging out the prices they are paying for used bikes. Blue books are available to the public; however, they are expensive and, for a variety of reasons, may not be completely accurate. They will provide a good general price range though.

Another, and perhaps the most practical, way for most of us to get an idea of what a bike is worth is simply watching the classifieds, either in the local newspapers or in dedicated motorcycle magazines, such as *Walneck's Classifieds* (sic) or *Classic Bike*.

After a few weeks you'll get a very good idea of what a particular model is worth. For example if the going rate for R75/5s seems to run between $2,500 and $3,500, then you'll know that the one advertised as "mint" for $1,500 is either the bargain of a lifetime or a gross misrepresentation. Of course you can always subscribe to the philosophy of the die-hard motorcycle collector—"I wanted it, he had it, I paid what he asked for it." Maybe not the best plan from an economic point of view, but one that does work.

THE PRACTICAL BMW BUYER'S GUIDE CHECKLIST

The following checklist will make inspecting and assessing a used bike a lot easier. To avoid writing in this book, make a photocopy and take it with you to the seller's place. After running through the list, tally up your findings, compare the pros and cons, and mull over the asking price. If it seems like the bike for you, go for it; if not, move on.

Equipment to bring with you:
Small flashlight—useful for looking into those dark deep places.
Small mechanic's mirror—ditto
Notebook and pen
Clean rag—you'll probably want to wipe your hands off afterward
Tire pressure gauge—a good, safe ride requires proper inflation

Overall condition (Mom always said that first impressions are the most lasting)**:**
In general . . .
Is the bike complete?
Does it look well maintained?
Do the frame and engine numbers match?

If the bike is an older model or a collectible, are the numbers correct for the year and model?
Does it include any accessories or original versions of updated parts?

Simple stuff:
Do the lights, horn, and switches all work properly?
Are there any signs of crash damage or other abuse?
    (Use your mirror to look under the fuel tank,
        fenders and behind the fairing.)
Are the cables and hoses in good shape?
Is the brake-fluid level correct?
If you have any doubt that the engine, transmission, and rear end oils are not topped off, check them before starting and riding the bike.
Do all the controls work smoothly?

Running gear:
Check the frame for flaking paint, rust, or cracks.
Check the centerstand mounts on /5 /6 and /7 models.
Is the fork straight?
Do the fork seals leak?
Does the fork move smoothly?
Are the steering head bearings dented, loose, or overly tight?

Moving to the rear of the bike . . . :

Are there any visible and obvious signs of damage, such as gross wheel misalignment or a twisted swing arm?

Any play in the swing arm?

Any wheel bearing play?

Do the rear shocks leak oil? (Caution: Maybe the shocks are just bone dry 'cause all of the oil leaked out—a rare occurrence, but it does happen.)

Is there any play in the linkage, and are the bolts tight?

Wheels, rims and brakes:

Are the tires dry-rotted?

Is there any tread left?

Are the rims dented or dinged?

Are any spokes broken, twisted or bent?

Is the tire pressure correct?

Does the front wheel spin freely?

Are the front wheel bearings in good shape?

Is there any life left in the brake pads (disc)?

Is there any adjustment left on the brake rod or cable (drum)?

Engine and transmission:

Are there any oil leaks?

Does the engine make odd noises?

Does the engine start easily?

Does it settle down to a regular idle?

Does it respond to the throttle?

Does it smoke?

Is there a rattle coming from the gearbox/engine junction (indicating a dry input shaft spline)?

Any leaks from the rear of the transmission cover or rear end?

R25, R26, R27 (1950-1966)

Chapter 2

The Early Singles

In my misspent youth, I looked at all BMW singles with disdain. I saw them then as overpriced and slow, particularly compared to the quarter-liter bikes of the day that were coming from Japan. Now I look at them for what they really are—well-constructed, expertly engineered, jewel-like motorcycles that are slow. By and large, they make fun bikes. They are nice Sunday runabouts and should prove fairly reliable as long as they aren't thrashed too hard.

There are a few drawbacks to owning a single. First is the limited power output, which ranges from a paltry 12 horsepower (R25) to a slightly less paltry 18 (R27). As you can imagine, acceleration is leisurely, and running one on the highway is foolhardy. The second consideration is parts pricing. Since the single is nothing less than one half of a 500-cc twin, many of the parts are common to both. As such, the prices are, in most cases, identical. In some cases, parts peculiar to the single are harder to come by and more expensive than the equivalent part used on a twin.

All that said, any of the singles—particularly one of those covered here—can make a nice practical classic if you don't need the bike for highway travel. They are certainly worth owning, if only because they are so quietly elegant.

R25 (1950–1956)

The R25 was the first "modern" BMW to leave the factory after World War II. Introduced in 1950 as a successor to the R24, which was really a prewar design, the R25 featured a welded steel frame, plunger rear suspension, and a 12-horsepower overhead valve engine. Distinctive features included a heavily valanced front fender, tank-top toolbox and beehive taillight. The seat was a simple rubber pan, suspended by a vertical coil spring.

A variation on the R25 was the R25/2, which made its appearance in 1951. Minor improvements included an updated front fender that utilized bolted-on stays, as opposed to the previous version's riveted braces, and a modified seat-mounting assembly with a cantilever-style mounting bracket.

In 1953, the R25/3 replaced the /2 version. Updates included a 13-horsepower engine (hold'er Newt, she's gonna buck!) and redesigned styling. Hydraulically damped front forks replaced the previous model's undamped spring front end. Wheel hubs became full width, and the wheels themselves were interchangeable.

R26 (1955–1960)

Now we're talking. In my opinion the R26 is a much better bet as a rider than any of the 25s. The R26 was almost a complete redesign of the older model. The suspension was completely revamped. In the rear, a swing arm replaced the old plunger style units. Up front, an Earles fork was bolted on. Engine upgrades included larger cylinder-head fins, a 2-millimeter bigger carburetor—26-millimeter as compared to the previous bike's 24-millimeter unit—and an upgraded air inlet. The drive shaft now ran in an enclosed tube that was part of the swing arm. The end result was a faster, better handling bike than the one that came before it. Styling was also modernized: Parts were much cleaner looking than on the R25, and the front fender lost its valance, although the fuel tank regained its top-loading toolbox.

R27 (1960–1966)

The final incarnation of the single was also the longest-lived, and in my opinion it is the best of the singles. The engine received the most attention. Horsepower was upgraded to 18 at 7,400 rpm. At the same time, a spring-loaded cam chain tensioner was installed to damp out unwanted chain vibrations. Because the engine shook a little more, it was rubber mounted into the slightly modified R26 frame. As a rider, the R27 is the most practical. It's quick enough to keep up with most traffic, is the most reliable of the singles, and is the easiest to find parts for.

BMW Buyers Guide Spec Sheet—R25/3 (1953–1958)

Engine type	Overhead valve, pushrod single
Displacement	247 cc
Compression ratio	7:1
Ignition	Battery and coil
Carburetion	24-millimeter Bing
Horsepower	13 bhp
Lighting	6-volt, battery and generator
Transmission	4-speed foot shift with "mechanics" hand shift/neutral finder
Curb weight	330 lbs
Instruments	Speedometer, neutral light indicator, charge indicator
Frame	Double downtube, welded construction
Suspension	Hydraulically damped telescopic fork, plunger rear.
Wheel size	3.25 × 18 front and rear
0–60	n/a
Standing-start 1/4 mile	24 seconds
Top speed	74 mph

BMW Buyers Guide Spec Sheet—R26 (1955–1960)

Engine type ———————— Overhead valve, pushrod single
Displacement   ———————— 247 cc
Compression ratio ————— 7.5:1
Ignition ———————————— Battery and coil
Carburetion ——————————— 26-millimeter Bing
Horsepower ————————— 15 bhp @ 6,400 rpm
Lighting ——————————— 6-volt, battery and generator
Transmission ——————— 4-speed, foot shift
Curb weight   ————————— 348 lbs
Instruments   ——————— Speedometer, neutral light, charge indicator
Frame —————————————— Double downtube, welded construction
Suspension ——————————— Earles front fork, rear swing arm.
Wheel size   ——————————— 3.25 × 18 front and rear
0–60 ———————————————— 20.4* seconds
Standing start 1/4 mile — 20.5* seconds (62 miles per hour)
Top speed ——————————— 80 mph
*Take these figures with a large grain of salt.

BMW Buyers Guide Spec Sheet—R27 (1960–1966)

Engine type ——————————— Overhead valve, pushrod vertical single
Displacement   ———————— 247 cc
Compression ratio ————— 8.2:1
Ignition ———————————— Battery and coil
Carburetion ———————————— 26-millimeter Bing
Horsepower ————————— 18 bph @ 7,400 rpm
Lighting ——————————— 6-volt, battery and generator
Transmission ——————— 4-speed
Curb weight   ————————— 360 lbs
Instruments   ——————— Speedometer, neutral light, charge indicator
Frame —————————————— Double down tube, welded construction
Suspension ——————————— Earles fork, rear swing arm
Wheel size   ——————————— 3.25 × 18 front and rear
0–60 ———————————————— 21.5 seconds*
Standing start 1/4 mile — 21.5 seconds*
Top speed ——————————— 84 mph*
*as tested by *Cycle World* in May 1964

What They Said at the Time

"The R25/3 is no ordinary motorcycle." *Motor Cycle*, February 1956

"[The R26]—a quiet, lively, and economical roadster with first class springings, steering, and braking, and a high standard of finish." *Motor Cycling*, April 1959

"The R27 will take a beating without complaint. The rider's enjoyment of breeze and scenery will not be disturbed by excessive vibration or exhaust noise." *Cycle World*, May 1964

R25 air filter now has a separate housing.

Check rear plunger suspension (R25).

Charging, may be problematic.

Fork gaiters may split at seams (R25).

Front fender riveted to stays (R25).

Earles forks may not have grease fittings; if not pay close attention to the bearings.

Rubber engine mounts may be worn out.

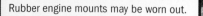

No more hand shift. Make certain the catch works on the oddball sidestand.

R67, R68, R51/2, R51/3 (1950-1956)

Chapter 3

Rebirth of the Twin

The R51/2 was BMW's first postwar twin cylinder model. Announced in early December 1949, the first 1,000 units were earmarked for the French police. (You'd have thought they'd have had their fill of German motorcycles rolling through their streets by then!) During the 1950 season, the bikes were released to eager customers around the world. While the design was based on the prewar R51, there were some changes. Conventional 7/8-inch handlebars replaced the old 1-inch version and the old-style inverted levers were dropped. Front forks now had two-way damping, although the plunger rear suspension was retained. Although the bike certainly proved that BMW was capable of making a comeback, it was a dated design, especially the engine, which was the prewar powerplant with its twin chain-driven cams.

In February 1951, BMW debuted a new model. The R51/3 looked much like its predecessor; however it had what amounted to a brand new engine, housed in the old cycle parts. The new engine had a single cam mounted high in the crankcase. The old wear-prone cam chain was dropped. A series of spur gears now drove the cam and oil pump, which was located directly beneath the crankshaft. The generator was moved from the top of the engine to the end of the crankshaft. The auto-advance unit and breaker points were located at the end of the crankshaft. Four-ring pistons were used, and the valve adjusters were located at the pushrod end of the rocker arm. New for BMW was a neutral switch installed in the transmission; this operated an indicator light in the headlight.

The R67 600-cc model also became available during 1951. Built primarily for sidecar use, it was a rather pedestrian affair. In fact it, was little more than a big-bore version of the R51/3, and as such, all of the cycle parts were iden-

tical. Performance issues were rectified with the release of the R67/2, which had somewhat more horsepower and was altogether a much livelier machine. Running changes to the R67/2 model included an air filter with a sliding choke lever and a twin leading shoe front brake.

Announced in 1951, but not released until the summer of 1952, the R68 was the top of the line BMW sports/roadster. The forerunner of the R69 sports model, the R68 had 35 horsepower at 7 grand, full-width hubs with a twin leading shoe front brake, and alloy rims. The telescopic front fork had two-way damping, but the rear suspension was still by plunger.

What They Said at the Time

BMW Buyers Guide Spec Sheet—R51/2 (1950)

Engine type ——————— Overhead valve, flat twin
Displacement ———— 494 cc
Compression ratio ——— 6.3:1
Ignition ——————— Battery and coil
Carburetion ————— Dual Bing slide carburetors (22-millimeter)
Horsepower ————— 24 bhp @ 5,800 rpm
Lighting ——————— Bosch 6-volt, generator
Transmission ———— 4-speed, hand clutch
Curb weight ———— 419 lbs
Instruments ———— Speedometer
Frame ——————— Welded steel cradle
Suspension ————— Telescopic front fork, plunger rear suspension
Wheel size ————— 3.00 × 19 front, 3.50 × 19 rear
0–60 ——————— n/a
Standing start 1/4 mile — 19.8 seconds @ 65 miles per hour
Top speed ————— 88 mph

BMW Buyer's Guide Spec Sheet—R51/3 (1951–1954)

Engine type ———— Overhead valve, flat twin
Displacement ———— 490 cc
Compression ratio ——— 6.3:1
Ignition ——————— Norris magneto
Carburetion ————— Dual 22-millimeter Bings
Horsepower ————— 24 bhp @ 5,800 rpm
Lighting ——————— 6 volt
Transmission ———— 4-speed
Curb weight ———— 419 lbs
Instruments ———— Speedometer, neutral light
Frame ——————— Welded steel cradle
Suspension ————— Telescopic front fork, plunger rear suspension
Wheel size ————— 3.00 × 19 front, 3.50 × 19 rear
0–60 ——————— n/a
Standing start 1/4 mile — 16.8 seconds @ 76 miles per hour
Top speed ————— 90 mph

BMW Buyer's Guide Spec Sheet—R67–R67/2

Engine type ——————— Overhead valve, flat twin
Displacement ———————— 590 cc
Compression ratio ————— 5.6:1 (R67), 5.6:1 (R67/2)
Ignition ——————————— Norris magneto
Carburetion ——————————— Dual Bing 24-millimeter slide carburetors
Horsepower ——————————— 26 bhp @ 5,500 rpm (R67), 28 bhp @ 5,600 rpm (R67/2)
Lighting ——————————— Norris 6 volt
Transmission ——————— 4-speed
Curb weight ———————— 423 lbs
Instruments ——————————— Speedo, neutral light, charge indicator
Frame ——————————— Welded steel cradle
Suspension ——————————— Telescopic fork, plunger rear suspension
Wheel size ————————— 3.00 × 19 front, 3.50 × 19 rear
0–60 ——————————— n/a
Standing start 1/4 mile — n/a
Top speed ————————— 90 mph

BMW Buyer's Guide Spec Sheet—R68 (1952–1954)

Engine type ——————— Overhead valve, flat twin
Displacement ———————— 594 cc
Compression ratio —————— 7.5:1
Ignition ———————————— Norris magneto
Carburetion ———————— Dual 26-millimeter Bing slide carburetors
Horsepower ——————————— 35 bhp @ 7,000 rpm
Lighting ——————————— 6 volt Norris
Transmission ———————— 4-speed
Curb weight ———————— 425 pounds
Instruments ———————— Speedometer, neutral light, charge indicator
Frame ——————————— Welded steel cradle
Suspension ————————— Telescopic front fork, plunger rear suspension
Wheel size ————————— 3.00 × 19 front, 3.50 × 19 rear
0–60 —————————————— n/a
Standing start 1/4 mile — n/a
Top speed ———————— 100 mph

Parts may be expensive and difficult to find.

Valve covers should be of the two-piece, prewar design, on the R51/2.

Cam chains are a weak point.

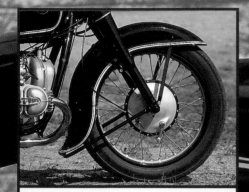
Should have metal dust covers on front fork.

As with all roller engines, beware of plugged oil slingers.

33

R50, R60, R69 (1955–1960)

Chapter 4
The Best Motorcycles in the World?

In 1955, BMW ushered in a new level of motorcycling sophistication, the likes of which had never been seen before. The new models, christened the R50 (500 cc), the R60 (600 cc) and the R69 (600 cc, sport tuning) were superbly built, comfortable, reliable, and while not the fastest bikes on the road, gave a good account of themselves. The engines were slightly modified single-cam units as previously used in R51/3–R67 and R68 models, although with some detail improvements made mainly to increase power. What really set the new models apart was the adoption of rear swing arm suspension and the innovative Earles front fork.

The swing arm frame was entirely new, very substantial, and as well made as any of its predecessors. As modern then as it sounds now, the rear suspension featured hydraulic shock absorbers, with preload adjustable springs, and it pivoted on adjustable, tapered roller bearings. The front suspension was a leading link type of fork designed by Englishman Ernie Earles, but subtly modified by BMW. Like the rear swing arm, the front pivot arm rode on tapered roller bearings, and wheel travel was damped by hydraulic shock absorbers. However, the front suspension had no provision for preload adjustment. Wheel diameter was reduced to 18 inches front and rear, although the tire widths remained as before, 3.00 and 3.50 inches respectively.

The new engines were tweaked to provide somewhat more horsepower. Presumably the extra power was required because the new chassis weighed slightly more than the old version. This extra power was transferred to the transmission through a new automotive-type diaphragm spring, single-plate clutch in place of the old single-plate, multispring unit. A new three-shaft transmission was employed, as was a new type of drive shaft with a sliding coupling—the last a necessity brought on by the increased suspension travel of the new model.

Of the three new models, the R69 was the flagship. With its "ton up" performance, it was one of the most competent motorcycles of its time, and it soon developed a reputation as a real road burner.

What They Said at the Time

BMW Buyer's Guide Spec Sheet—R50, R60, R69 (1955–1960)

Engine type ———————— Overhead valve flat twin
Displacement ———————— 490 cc (R50), 590 cc (R60 and R69)
Compression ratio ——— 6.8:1 (R50), 6.5:1 (R60), 8:1 (R69)
Ignition ———————— Norris magneto
Carburetion ———————— Dual 24 Bing slide Carburetors (R50 & R60), 26-millimeter (R69)
Horsepower ———————— 26 bhp @ 5,800 rpm (R50), 28 bhp @ 5,600 rpm (R60), 35 bhp @ 6,800 rpm (R69)
Lighting ———————— 6 volt Norris, generator
Transmission ———————— 4-speed
Curb weight ———————— 429 lbs (R50 and R60), 445 lbs (R69)
Instruments ———————— Speedometer w/tripmeter, neutral light, ignition warning light
Frame ———————— Welded steel cradle
Suspension ———————— Earles front fork and rear swing arm
Wheel size ———————— 3.00 × 18 front, 3.50 × 18 rear
0–60 ———————— n/a (R50), 7.8 (R60), 7.0 (R69)
Standing start 1/4 mile—— 16.8 seconds @ 76 miles per hour (R50), 16.2 seconds @ 79 miles per hour (R60), 15.5 seconds @ 85 miles per hour (R69).
Top speed ———————— 85 mph (R50), 90 mph (R60), 102 mph (R69)

Odd handling may mean that the front fork pivot is in the sidecar position.

No grease fittings on front swing arm means bearings are prone to wear and water damage.

Magneto may be headed south; get the bike good and hot during the test ride

Original engine design includes nonrotating valves—these have probably been replaced by now; if not, consider doing so at the earliest opportunity.

Still a chance that those slinger rings will pack up.

R50, R60/2 (1960-1969)

Chapter 5
The Slash 2 Models

Arguably the best-recognized and the most practical of all the vintage BMWs, the slash 2 series R50 and R60 make fine everyday riders. They are also highly sought-after collectibles. In truth, the two models differ little from the previous incarnations. First shown in 1960 and released to the market in 1961, the slash two versions incorporated strengthened camshafts and crankshafts and a broader taper on the crankshaft to better support the generator rotor. The R60/2 acquired a bit more compression, which upped the horsepower to an even 30 at 5,800 rpm. In 1967, an optional telescopic front fork was offered. Buyers resisted bikes with this option, dubbed the U.S. model, and today bikes so equipped bring slightly less money than a comparable Earles fork-equipped version—ironic, since the telescopic option added $36 to the price of an R50 and $12 to the price of an R60 (according to the Butler and Smith price list, effective March 9, 1968). During the 1967 model year, the sidecar lugs were deleted from the frame, presumably because the U.S. fork wasn't up to the stresses imposed by sidecar use, and sidecar sales in general had reached a low ebb. Both models came standard with a 4.5-gallon fuel tank, while a 6.25-gallon tank was an option, as was a larger dual seat. Standard paint was of course black, with white as an option.

What They Said at the Time

"The R50 (/2) stands out from the ruck as a superb tourer for the connoisseur." *Motorcycle*, September 1953

"Smooth, swift, silent." *Motorcycle Mechanics*, October 1964

BMW Buyer's Guide Spec Sheet—R50/2, R60/2

Engine type ———————— Overhead valve, flat twin

Displacement ——————— 490 cc (R50/2), 590 cc (R60/2)

Compression ratio —————— 68:1 (R50/2), 7.5:1 (R60/2)

Ignition ———————————— Norris magneto

Carburetion ————————— Dual 24-millimeter Bing slide carburetors (both models)

Horsepower ————————— 28 bhp @ 5,800 (R50/2), 30 bhp @ 5.800 (R60/2)

Lighting ————————————— Norris generator

Transmission ——————— 4 speed

Curb weight ———————— 430 pounds (R50/2 &R60/2)

Instruments ———————— Speedometer, neutral indicator, charge indicator.

Frame ———————————— Double downtube, steel cradle

Suspension ————————— Earles front fork, rear swing arm

Wheel size ————————— 3:00 × 18 front, 3:50 × 18 rear

0-60 ————————————— n/a (R50/2), 7.8 seconds (R60/2)

Standing start 1/4 mile — 17 seconds @ 75 miles per hour (R50/2), 16.2 seconds @ 79 miles per hour (R60/2)

Top speed ———————— 84 miles per hour (R50/2), 90 miles per hour (R60/2)

The Magneto can pack it in without much notice.

As with all roller bearing engines, over-loaded slinger rings can be a problem.

Early models (pre-1965) have no grease fitting on front swing arm; be aware of possible rust/bushing seizure.

R50S, R69S (1960-1969)

Chapter 6
Vintage Hot Rods

Arguably the most desirable of the late Earles fork models, the S series bikes were intended to become the company's performance flagships. The R69S succeeded, becoming the most popular of the pre-1970 BMWs sold in the United States (1960–1969 over 11,000 bikes). The R50S developed a rather poor reputation, at least for a BMW, and was withdrawn after a brief model run of two years and only 1,634 units (1960–1962).

Externally, few differences distinguished the S series from its pedestrian siblings. The 600-cc version bore the legend R69S emblazoned on its rear fender in the form of a cast chrome-plated piece of script. The R50S had no such emblem to identify it as being any different from a run-of-the-mill slash 2. The external differences were the addition of hydraulic steering dampers and large finned exhaust nuts, both of which could obviously be fitted to any of the other models in the line-up. Larger air filters and mufflers were also part of the S package, and discernible to the sharp eyed. As you surmise, it wouldn't be hard at all to counterfeit either model, at least externally.

R50S

Internally it was a different story. The R50 engine was upgraded to S specs by raising the compression to 9.5:1 and opening up the intake ports. Larger 28-millimeter exhaust valves were also fitted. Bigger 26-millimeter Bing carburetors replaced the standard 24-millimeter versions. A new set of gearbox ratios was also developed. Though not exactly a close-ratio box, the gear set at least allowed the engine to be kept on the boil. Horsepower went up to 35 at 7,650 rpm. But as horsepower and performance went up, reliability dropped.

The big problem was crankshaft flex. This had been negligible in the R50, which topped out at 5,800 rpm, but became a real issue when the same crank was spun up to 7,650. A crankshaft-mounted vibration damper was installed in front of the generator, but it really didn't do the job. The real solution was to replace the standard rear main bearing with a spherical roller-type bearing. The new bearing didn't prevent crankshaft flex, but it wasn't destroyed by it either. As the crank wobbled around in the cases, the bearing wobbled with it. Unfortunately for BMW, the R50S was expensive compared to the other bikes in its class, most of which offered better performance and reliability. At the end of 1962 the R50S was withdrawn from the market.

R69S

The R69S faired much better. It was expensive by the standards of the day, but not so much more than its rivals. It also had very good performance, and was extremely reliable—at least when the pilot kept the rpm within reasonable sight of the redline and changed the oil on a regular basis. BMW sold lots and lots of the things; in fact, in the United States it soon became the most popular model. In 1967 the telescopic fork became available as an option, though most bikes continued to be sold with the Earles fork.

What They Said at the Time

"[The R69S is] a near perfect machine." *Cycle World*, September 1965

BMW Buyer's Guide Spec Sheet— R50S (1960–1962), R69S (1960–1969)

Engine type —————— Overhead valve, flat twin

Displacement ——————— 490 cc (R50S), 590 cc (R69S)

Compression ratio ——— 9.2:1 (R50S), 9.5:1 (R69S)

Ignition ——————————— Bosch magneto

Carburetion —————————— Dual 26-millimeter Bing slide carburetors (both models)

Horsepower —————————— 35 bhp @ 7,650 RPM (R50S), 42 bhp @ 7,000 RPM

Lighting —————————— 6-volt, generator

Transmission ————————— 4-speed

Curb weight ————————— 430 lbs (R50S), 445 lbs (R69S)

Instruments ————————— Speedometer, ignition warning light (charging indicator), neutral indicator. Optional-VDO tachometer.

Frame —————————— Double cradle welded steel

Suspension —————————— Earles front fork and swing arm rear suspension. From 1967, telescopic front forks were an option on the R69S.

Wheel size ————————— 2.15 × 18 front, 3.50 × 18 rear

0–60 ——————————— 7.6 seconds (R69S), n/a (R50S)*

Standing start 1/4 mile —— 16.2 seconds (R69S), n/a(R50S)*

Top speed ————————— 109 mph (R69S), 105 mph (R50S)*

*Take these with a grain of salt. Like all of the performance stats, these figures were taken from period tests.

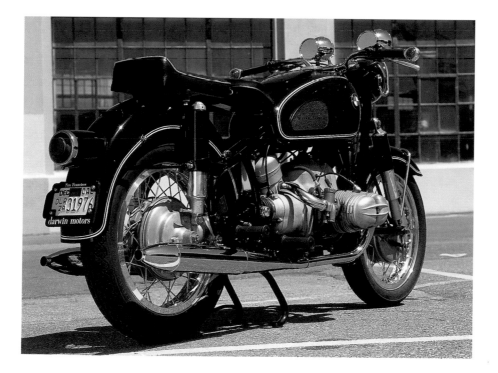

A popular conversion mates a 12-style chassis with later engines. When done properly, these converted motorcycles are highly functional but not as valuable as motorcycles with correct engines.

R50S—limited production, watch for counterfeits.

Engine vibration may be due to a worn-out vibration damper; these are relatively cheap and are easy to replace.

Make sure the steering damper is fitted; make doubly certain that the thing still works.

As with all /2s, the slingers may be full. If the engine has been overhauled, make certain that the rear main bearing is correct.

R50/5, R60/5, R75/5 (1969-1975)

Chapter 7

The Slash 5 Models

By the mid-1960s the writing was on the cylinder wall. BMW's motorcycles, as good as they were, appealed to a limited and shrinking customer base. Lighter and arguably sportier motorcycles from Japan, the Continent, and England were putting a serious dent in BMW's order book. The new bikes, particularly the Japanese models, rivaled and in some cases exceeded, BMW's hard-won reputation for dependability. They combined excellent performance and reliability, with a lower price tag. As a bonus they were available in colors other than black and white.

Don't think for a moment that BMW's managers missed any of this. They didn't, and were hard at work developing new models that would meet the challengers head on. In 1964, BMW equipped its ISDT entries with a prototype frame and long-travel telescopic forks. The front-end went into production shortly thereafter, becoming available as the optional U.S. fork. The frame, which owed more than a passing nod to the Norton Featherbed design, was held in reserve until the new engine, being developed concurrently, was thoroughly tested and found suitable.

The new models, the slash five series, were introduced to the public at the Cologne Motorcycle Show in September 1969. Although they were instantly recognizable as BMWs, they bore little in common with their predecessors, save the basic design.

The slash 5 engines were built in three capacities, 500 cc, 600 cc and 750 cc. All shared the same bottom end. Only the cylinders, pistons, and heads were changed to suit. The R50 was equipped with a kick-starter only—electric start was an option. The R60 and R75 had both a kick-starter and electric starter. The R50 and R60 came through with traditional Bing slide carburetors; the R75 used new-fangled, and initially troublesome, Bing constant velocity carburetors. These new "vacuum" carburetors tended to stick at inopportune moments—fortunately most of the problems were resolved within a few months of the bike's release via update kits supplied by BMW.

Technically, the new motors were far superior to any that came before them. Though outwardly they bore a passing resemblance to the slash 2 series, internally it was a brand new ballgame.

For starters, there was now a plain bearing crank, complete with a high-pressure lubrication system and replaceable oil filter. No more troublesome slinger rings waiting to cause mischief. The other big change was that the camshaft was now positioned below the crankshaft. Since the change moved the pushrod tubes under the engine, it made for a cleaner overall appearance. There was also a case to be made that lubrication of the cam lobes was enhanced, although cam lobe wear had never been a problem on the older models.

Running gear was all new and designed with weight savings in mind. The fenders were fiberglass—they didn't rust, bust, bend, or corrode. The frame was composed of a welded-up front half—the back bone being an especially strong and light length of oval tubing—with a lightweight, bolted-on rear subsection. Early rear frames had a hole bored through them where the taillight wires passed through. These sometimes caused the rear section to crack. Since the section broke behind the shock mount, no real harm was done, and owners either welded up the break, or replaced the subframe. The rims were aluminum alloy, 18 inch in the rear and 19 in the front; drum brakes were fitted fore and aft.

Instrumentation included a tachometer and a full array of warning lights. A friction steering damper was standard equipment, and under the seat was the most comprehensive toolkit ever seen on a motorcycle. The old-fashioned plunger style key was retained as a connection to the past, if nothing else.

Problems with the new model were few, and for the most part, far between. Outside of the ones mentioned, only two others are worth discussing. First, early slash fives, particularly the 750s, which could really hum, sporadically developed a bad case of the high-speed wobbles. The problem was exacerbated when high U.S.-style handlebars were used or a handlebar-mounted fairing installed. Initially, stiffer fork springs were issued. Starting with the 1973 model year, the swing arm was lengthened by 50 millimeters, which for the most part eliminated any further high-speed drama, and also provided some extra room for a larger battery.

Second was a problem that would reappear off and on for many years. Some bikes developed inexplicable rear main seal leaks. Eventually this was traced to ring seating problems caused by overly gentle break-in procedures. New owners, particularly older ones, and most particularly those who were acutely aware that they had just bought one of the most expensive motorcycles in the world, tended to break in their bikes very gently—perhaps too gently. This caused the piston rings to glaze over. Once the rings glazed, combustion gases leaked passed the rings and pressurized the crankcase. This was compounded by the basic design, which had both pistons reaching BDC together, which reduced crankcase volume. The compressed gases had nowhere to go, so they exited via the rear main seal, usually taking a few drops of oil. Various rear main seals were tried, which worked with varying degrees of success. Once the real culprit became known, the problem didn't exactly vanish but it was greatly reduced. The solution was simple: Dealers were advised to prep new bikes with a light break-in oil, and run the dickens out of them before delivery to the customer.

Overall the new line-up was well received, particularly by the motorcycle press. If there was any real controversy, it was over styling—particularly on the 1972 and up "toaster tank" models. In a bid to win over the American market, BMW decided a splash of chrome was in order. Accordingly, the 1972-1973 models had chrome side panels fitted over the battery, and chrome inserts bolted to the standard 18-liter fuel tank; the optional 24-liter tank still had the traditional rubber pads. I liked the new look enough to buy a brand new R60/5. Not everyone else felt the same way, and for the 1974 model year the chrome was quietly deleted.

While the slash 5 series machines have their foibles, all are easily corrected. They make terrific day-to-day riders and have the added cachet of being somewhat collectible. All in all a sensible motorcycle that's perfect for the novice BMW rider, restorer or collector.

What They Said at the Time

"BMW has made a bold risk bid for the performance buyer. Will a flat twin as big as the R75 really handle? Take a ride baby—you'll see." *Cycle,* November 1969

"The R60 somehow manages to feel light and responsive, yet rock steady, all at the same time. The machine goes where you aim it." *Cycle,* November 1970

"[The BMW R50/5 is] Still smooth, still relaxing, still superb." *Motorcycle Mechanics,* July 1973

BMW Buyer's Guide Spec Sheet—
R50/5, R60/5, R75/5

Engine type ————————— Overhead value, flat twin

Displacement ———————— 494 cc (R50), 599 cc (R60), 745 cc (R75)

Compression ratio ————— 8.6:1 (R50), 9.2:1(R60), 9.0:1 (R75)

Ignition ————————————— Battery and coil

Carburetion —————————— Dual 26-millimeter Bing slide carburetors (R50 and R60), dual 32-millimeter constant velocity Bing carburetors (R75)

Horsepower ———————————— 36 bhp @ 6,600 rpm (R50), 46 bhp @ 6,600 rpm (R60), 57 bhp @ 6,400 (R75)

Lighting ——————————————— 12-volt, alternator

Transmission ———————————— 4-speed, shaft drive

Curb weight —————————————— 408 lbs (R50), 420 lbs (R60), 437 lbs (R75)

Instruments ——————————————— Speedometer, tachometer, neutral light, high-beam indicator, charging indicator, directional indicator

Frame ——————————————————— Welded steel duplex with bolt-on rear section

Suspension ———————————————— Telescopic front fork with swing arm rear suspension

Wheel size ————————————————— 3.25 × 19 front, 4.00 × 18 rear

0–60 ——————————————————————— 9.8 seconds (R50), 5.9 seconds (R60), 6.2 seconds (R75)*

*R75 final gearing was slightly higher

Standing start 1/4 mile —— 16 seconds (R50), 15.57 (R60), 13.55 seconds (R75)

Top speed ——————————————— 90 mph (R50), 102.7 mph (R60), 109 mph (R75)

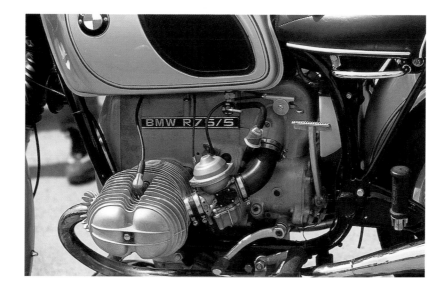

Every slash five that I've ever been on has had a shivery tach needle. Some are worse than others. The tachometer can be rebuilt if it's a real problem.

Early models had no fuses in the main wiring harness; most of these have been upgraded by now, but it never hurts to ask.

A ratchetlike feel at the twist grip indicates worn twist-grip gears.

Slash 5s tend to make a bit of top end noise. That clatter may mean the valves need adjusting or that rocker arm side play is excessive and needs adjusting. The rocker arms originally came with plain bushings; these were upgraded to needle bearings in subsequent models and many /5s have had the needle bearings retrofitted.

Center stands tend to wear, as do the frame stops. When the center stand is deployed, both wheels should balance off the ground.

Soft fork springs were a chronic /5 problem.

Lurching or sudden clutch engagement means the input shaft is dry or requires shimming.

The 1970 and 1971 models have no covers over the battery, nor should there be clips on the frame to hold the covers. Lots of rear frame sections were replaced, though, so the presence of clips doesn't necessarily mean the covers should be there.

The 1972 and 1973 models should have a long swing arm. You can actually see the extension welded in place at the end of the drive shaft tube.

Rear wheel splines occasionally wear out, usually due to poor maintenance. Check the splines by rocking the wheel against the coupling or removing it and physically inspecting the splines.

Kickstand bosses tend to break every so often; also make sure the boss isn't seized to the stand and spinning in the frame.

Check the rear main seal for oil leaks—they should all have been fixed by now, but who knows? There may be a few out there that are still weeping.

R90/6, R75/6, R60/6 (1974–1976)

Chapter 8
The Slash Sixes

The introduction of the slash 5 series, particularly the R75, put BMW on the map as a manufacturer of serious, high-performance motorcycles, especially in the United States. The slash 5 series were good solid motorcycles, and allowed BMW to dip a toe into the swirling waters of a burgeoning marketplace. But almost as soon as the new bikes hit the showroom floor, plans were afoot to update them.

Actually rumors of a 900-cc Über-bike had been floating around since the early 1960s, as had similar rumors of an R75 Sports model. BMW would squelch the rumors and build its first thoroughly modern motorcycles with the introduction of the slash 6 models in 1974.

While the slash 5s were a real improvement on the bikes that had come before them, some of the styling and engineering was still stuck in firmly in the 1960s. For starters, the front drum brake, good as it was, was still a drum brake. Likewise the four-speed transmission had grown obsolete. By 1970, all Japanese bikes came with at least five gears and some had six. Even Triumph offered a five-speed box by 1972. On the styling front, the slash five looked, well, dated. The headlight was a holdover from the 1950s, and the big tank, useful as it was, looked bulbous. The slash fives even used the same plunger-type key that BMW had been using for decades. It was a nice bow to tradition, but it meant that you needed two separate keys—one for the steering head-lock and seat, and one for the ignition. As a side issue, anyone with an ignition key could ride off on your new BMW.

On another front, the 750-cc class was no longer at the top of the performance hit parade. Actually by 1974 a 750-cc machine was starting to seem sedate; the 900-cc was the hot ticket, and if you didn't have one, or a model that could at least keep up with one, you were going to be stuck in second place.

To take back lost ground, BMW released the slash 6 models in 1974. There were to be four basic models: the new R90, the R90S, a revised R75, and the bargain basement R60. (The R50 was dropped from the line-up.) The R90S, a flagship version of the 900-cc model, was to tip the motorcycling world on its ear; however, such a significant model needs its own chapter, so we'll pass it by for the time being. Ostensibly the slash six line-up would address all of the shortcomings in the slash five line.

The six series looked much more modern. The old headlamp was replaced with a modern-looking unit that greatly improved the front-end appearance. It also picked up a quartz bulb that made it much more effective. The instruments were moved to a binnacle atop the steering head, along with a cluster of warning lights. The tachometer was now much larger, much steadier, and much more useful. A proper tumbler style key was positioned on the left side of the headlight. Unfortunately, it still didn't fit the seat and steering headlock, nor the optional locking fuel tank cap, meaning you had to carry at least two keys.

The small 4.5-gallon tank was used sans kneepads or chrome, although the larger 6.25-gallon tank was available as an option. The battery covers were now made of fiberglass, painted to match the tank and fenders. Mechanically, the big news was the addition of the 900-cc engine, a five speed 'box—common to all models—and a disc brake on the R75 and R90 models. The disc brake was pretty standard, save for one feature: the master cylinder was located under the fuel tank and a cable connected it to the lever. While this made it somewhat inconvenient to service, it did protect it from damage in the event of a mishap.

The new bikes, particularly the 900-cc versions, put BMW on the map as a maker of fast and easy-to-live-with motorcycles. Problems were few and far between, and what faults did crop up were easily put right. Today the slash six series bike has a well-deserved reputation as a workhorse of a motorcycle. And there are plenty of them to be found, which keeps the cost reasonable. While not as collectible as the slash five series, the R90S being the exception, the slash six series makes a much better all-around working bike. They are plenty quick, have decent brakes, and rarely break any expensive pieces.

What They Said at the Time

BMW Buyers Guide Spec Sheet—R60/6, R75/6, R90/6 (1974–1976)

Engine type —————— Overhead valve, flat twin

Displacement ——————— 599 cc (R60), 745 cc (R75), 898 cc (R90)

Compression ratio ———— 9.2:1 (R60), 9.0:1 (R75), 9.0:1 (R90)

Ignition —————————— Battery and coil

Carburetion —————————— Dual 26mm Bing slide carburetors (R60), dual 32mm constant velocity Bing carburetors (R75 and R90)

Horsepower* ——————— 40 bhp @ 6,500 rpm (R60), 50 bhp @ 6,500 rpm (R75), 60 bhp @ 6,500 rpm (R90)

Electrical system ——————— 12 volt alternator

Transmission —————————— 5-speed, shaft driven

Weight —————————— 441 lbs

Instruments ——————— Speedometer, tachometer, neutral light, high-beam indicator, charging indicator, directional indicator, low oil pressure indicator

Frame —————————— Welded steel duplex with bolted-on rear section

Suspension —————————— Telescopic front fork, swing arm rear

Tire size —————————— 3.25 × 19 front, 4.00 × 18 rear

0-60 —————————————— 7.5 seconds (R60), 6.0 seconds (R75), 5.0 seconds (R90)

Standing start 1/4 mile — 15.9 seconds (R60), 13.5 seconds (R75), 13.4 seconds (R90)

Top speed ————————— 103 mph (R60), 107 mph (R75), 112 mph (R90)

*DIN rating

Leaking rear main seal can be a problem, especially on R75-R90 models.

Standard rear shocks should be fitted with alloy covers.

Rear splines a problem.

Instruments housed in pod atop headlight.

Gaiters standard wear on front fork.

Drilled front disc brake makes a curious whirring sound—learn to live with it.

R60/6 continues with front drum brake, no hubcap fitted.

Centerstands and kickstands prone to wear and breakage.

Lurching trannys still a problem.

Some 900s' rims crack around spoke holes.

R90S (1973–1976) R100RS (1976–1984)

Chapter 9
BMW Gets Serious

Although BMW had been a serious player on the grand prix scene prior to World War II, it had been years since it had built anything that could be construed as a true performance motorcycle. Even the R69S, arguably its top-of-the-line hot rod during the 1960s, hadn't really been a serious contender when it came to flat-out speed.

True, the introduction of the slash five line had changed the public's perception of BMW. But while it was no longer seen only as a builder of conservative, somewhat stodgy machines, it certainly wasn't considered anything close to a superbike builder. This was despite the best efforts of the racing team of the American importer, Butler and Smith, and the team's inordinately talented and very brave rider, Reg Pridmore.

BMW knew that it needed a performance bike, one that embodied all of its traditional values, yet was capable of giving any motorcycle, at any time and at any place, a serious run for its money. The new model, the R90S, turned out to be not only a seriously competent motorcycle, but one that would become a milestone for both BMW and motorcycling in general.

Ostensibly released to celebrate BMW's 50th anniversary as a motorcycle manufacturer, the R90S model premiered in October 1973 at the Paris Motorcycle Show. The timing and location were no surprise. The Paris show of October 1923 had been the venue for the first showing of BMW's first motorcycle, the R32. The new model would change once and for all the idea that the Munich factory built only touring or semi-sporting "old men's motorcycles." The R90S was clearly the hit of the show and the most sensational model of 1974.

In performance, the R90S gave away nothing. Producing 67 horsepower at 7,000 rpm, the 440-pound (dry) sport bike was good for slightly over 125 miles per hour in dead stock trim.

Visually the bike was stunning. Dual front discs were fitted to a gaiterless fork. A small café racer styled fairing was mounted to the fork. The fairing contained a clock and voltmeter; it also proved to be surprisingly good at protecting the rider. The tank styling was reminiscent of the older 6-gallon version, sometimes seen on slash 2 models. An attractive dual seat was fitted, complete with a handsome tail fairing. Ever the practical manufacturer, BMW included a small storage space beneath the tail section. Low sport-type handlebars were used, as was a three-position hydraulic steering damper. From the outside, the engine looked standard, save for the black-painted cylinders and the dual 38-millimeter Dell'Orto "pumper" carburetors.

While the styling of the bike—a job done under contract by well-known designer Hans Muth—was stellar, it was the paint that really made it stand out. It was finished in a mind-bending smoke-gray, the likes of which had never been seen before. (Later bikes had a less attractive smoke-orange finish.) The smoke-gray paint was such a radical departure from what anyone else was doing that it stopped people in their tracks. Since the paint was hand applied, it meant that no two bikes were alike—an important sales feature on a bike that was the most expensive motorcycle in production. Although the R90S was available for only three short years, it catapulted BMW's image from maker of interesting touring bikes to cutting edge performance bike manufacturer. As an aside, it's worth noting that the R90S was more than just a pretty face. In 1976 the model managed to come home first at the Isle of Man Production Race and first and second at the Daytona Superbike race. To add icing to the cake, Pridmore and BMW would go on to win the 1976 AMA Superbike Championship.

R100RS

The R90S was a tough act to follow. Nonetheless BMW did, releasing a bike that was equally as groundbreaking, the R100RS. Introduced in late 1976 for the 1977 sales season, the R100RS was the first of the 1-liter BMWs. In its own way the RS was as radical a departure as the R90S, perhaps even more so. The engine now displaced a full 1,000 cc and made 70 horsepower. The styling was even more extreme than the R90S, which wasn't too surprising, given that the new model had also been penned by Muth. The bike featured a full roadrace-styled fairing, complete with a glass panel over the headlight. The handlebars dropped slightly below the top fork clamp. Oddly enough, they were fairly comfortable, and the faster you went, the more comfortable they became.

Initially the bike was offered with a three-quarter-length seat and tail fairing—a standard length R90S-style seat was available as an option. Surprisingly, passenger pegs came standard. Presumably anyone that could be persuaded to take the rear seat was indeed a very good friend. The bike was slated to have cast wheels from the get-go; unfortunately, delays in production meant that the first bikes were delivered with spoked wheels, highlighted with blue pinstriping around the edges. The engine received black-painted, squared-off valve covers. These were "handed," and mounting them the wrong way around gave the bike an odd look—accordingly, BMW marked them left and right or *Links* and *Recht* to avoid any confusion. (Eventually this was changed to an even simpler L and R.) Another external change was the return to Bing constant velocity carburetors. While the Dell'Ortos may have looked stylish and provided some modest increase in horsepower, they were, in fact, a bit finicky and difficult to keep in tune.

UPDATES (R100RS)

BMW churned out the twin-shock version of the R100RS from 1977 through 1984, a fairly long production run of eight years. During that time the bike saw numerous detail changes. Those changes, by year, include . . .

1978

Single key locking for the ignition, fork lock, seat, and gas cap.

Audible and extremely annoying turn-signal buzzer added; this was such a horrible idea that many buyers had them disconnected before leaving the showroom.

External linkage fitted to shifter to reduce shifting effort.

Steel cable lock inserted in the hollow frame backbone. (This was a dealer option on all other models.)

Mag wheels standard.

Rear disc brake standard.

Calipers no longer anodized blue.

Head and taillight now come on with ignition; no more headlight on/off switch.

Tachometer switched from cable operation to electronic.

Analog clock replaced by electric quartz version.

Green instrument lettering replaced by white.

A total of 200 special *Motorsport* editions offered; painted white with a red headlight surround.

1979

Hydraulic damper added to drive shaft.

Addition of a standard oil cooler.

Single row cam chain replaces the duplex version; the new chain has a master link to facilitate replacement and a spring-loaded, hydraulically damped tensioner.

Although points still fire the ignition, they are now incorporated in a separate housing that makes them much easier to set and ensures more accurate ignition timing.

Internally, a rerouting of the oil passages provides the rear main bearing with a more direct flow.

The dual seat and rear pegs became standard.

Conventional handlebar switches replace the odd BMW versions.

1980

Major changes include a pollution-reducing air intake system and lowered compression ratio (from 9.5:1 to 8.2:1) to allow use of unleaded fuel.

Federal law mandates standard 85-mile per hour speedometers; the one fitted to the RS is often binned by buyers for a more appropriate one from the parts book.

1981

This was a year of big changes.

"Galnikal" aluminum alloy cylinders reduce oil consumption, save weight and greatly improve cooling.

Electronic ignition standard.

Larger oil sump.

Exhaust now has two crossovers, one in front of the engine, one behind.

The clutch and flywheel weight is reduced by 40 percent, and clutch pull is reduced by 30 percent. The result is improved engine response, smoother shifting.

A new fork is used; travel remains the same, but BMW claims that the new version has better damping.

A stiffer swing arm, developed with the R80GS, replaces the old, flex-prone unit.

Diecast rear-end housing.

Frame improvements ease battery access.

A two-into-one carburetor cable system is now used.

The master cylinder migrates from beneath the fuel tank to the handlebar.

Brakes use new Brembo calipers.

1982

Saddlebags become standard equipment.

1983

No changes, but price drops from $7,025 (1982) to $6,500 (1983).

1984

This was the last gasp for the RS, now perceived as a somewhat over-the-hill, slightly underpowered sport/tourer. To mark the passing, BMW builds 250 pearl white versions and labels them "Last Edition."

What They Said at the Time

"BMW's R90S The World's Best Bike?" *Two Wheels*, November 1975

"Lavishly endowed with quality and the kind of performance that makes you wonder why everyone has to travel so slowly." *Cycle*, January 1976

"[The R100RS is] not black, it's not a friendly familiar face, it's not slow" *Cycle* December 1976

BMW Buyers Guide Spec Sheet— R90S (1973–1976), R100RS (1976–1984)

Engine type ———————— Overhead valve, flat twin

Displacement ———————— 898 cc (R90S), 980 cc (R100RS)

Compression ratio ————— 9.5:1 (R90S–R100RS), 8.2:1 (R100RS, 1980 and later)

Ignition ————————— Battery and coil, electronic ignition (R100RS, 1981 and later)

Carburetion ————————— Dual Dell'Orto 38mm slide carburetors with accelerator pumps (R90S only), dual 40mm Bing constant velocity carburetors (R100RS)

Horsepower* ———————— 65 bhp @ 6,600 rpm (R90S), 70 bhp @ 7,250 rpm (R100RS)

Electrical system ————— 12 volt alternator

Transmission —————— 5-speed, shaft driven

Weight: ————————— 425 lbs (R90S), 463 lbs (R100RS)

Instruments —————— Speedometer, tachometer, neutral light, high-beam indicator, charging indicator, directional indicator, low oil pressure light, low brake fluid light, clock, and voltmeter

Frame ———————— Welded steel, duplex cradle

Suspension ————— Telescopic front fork, swing arm rear

Tire size ————— 3.35 × 19 front, 4.00 × 18 rear

0-60 ————————— 4.5 seconds (R90S), 4.8 seconds (R100RS)

Standing start 1/4 miles ——— 13.0 seconds (R90S), 13.4 seconds (R100RS)

Top speed** ————— 125 mph (R90S), 122 mph (R100RS)

*DIN

**These were claimed figures.

Dell'Orto carburators on R90s can be tricky.

All common /5 and /6 problems still exist. In addition, be on the alert for cracked fairing panels, or bent brackets on the R100RS, particularly on the right-hand side. Since the right side lower panel complicates replacing the oil filter, flat rate mechanics tend to pry the fairing away rather than unbolt it.

R80/7, R100/7, R100/S, R100T (1977–1984)

Chapter 10

The Slash 7 Models

R80/7 TWIN-SHOCK VERSIONS (1977–1984)

Initially released in the United States for the 1978 season, the R80/7 was little more than an overbored R75/7. Essentially the bike was created for the European police market. The R75/7, with its 9:1 compression, demanded expensive, high-octane fuel. The Euro police forces wanted to burn something a bit less dear. BMW responded by overboring the R75 from 82 to 84.8 millimeters and dropping the compression to 8.0:1. The 50-horsepower R80 was a big hit with the Euro cops, who purchased thousands of the 800-cc workhorses.

In the United States, the R80 came with 8.5:1 com-

pression, endowing it with adequate, if not exactly sprightly, performance. Detail improvements included a modified shift-linkage assembly that was said to reduce shifting effort, and an electronic tachometer. In most other details the R80 was identical to the R75 it replaced. While the R80 was considered somewhat pedestrian in its day, it was, and still is, a very nice motorcycle, especially for those who want a "working classic." Maintenance requirements are low, and while the performance threshold is moderate, particularly by today's standards, the bike is fun to ride and has more than enough power to tour two-up.

R100/7 (1977–1978)
TWIN-SHOCK VERSIONS

For the enthusiast with a bit more cash to spend, the next step up was the R100/7. While visual differences between the 800-cc version and the full 1-liter bike were nonexistent, save for the displacement badge on the engine and side covers, the performance advantage of the 60-horsepower full 1,000-cc model was unmistakable.

R100S (1977–1978)

The R100S was either the red-headed stepchild of the S/RS lineup, or a very nice addition to it, depending on where you sit. Stylistically, the R100S looked nearly identical to the R90S, save for some detail changes. But the engine was a different story. The R100S was in a slightly softer state of tune and, despite having an additional 82 cc of displacement, was down two horsepower compared to the R90S. The loss of power was attributed to the R100S's CV-style Bing carburetors—rather than the Dell'Orto pump-type carbs on the R90S. Officially, BMW claimed that the Italian-made Dell'Ortos were troublesome and difficult to keep in tune, so it stopped using them. My guess is that BMW didn't want the S version of the R100 to be faster than its flagship RS model, so it intentionally detuned the S. Either way the R100S version is one of the nicer airheads. It looks the business and is very easy to tune and maintain. Besides, you can always fit a pair of Dell'Ortos, Mikunis, or flat-side Keihin's, if you want some trick gassers.

R100T (1979–1980)

The 100T was a gussied up replacement for the R100/7. It came with a dual front disc brake, although the first bikes were shipped with only one—dealers had to add the second. It also came with saddlebag mounts (the bags were an option), a clock and voltmeter, crash bars, and a fancy two-tone paint job. It was touted as a do-it-yourself platform for the touring rider or just a real nice basic motorcycle.

In 1979 both models received some long awaited updates. Since the inception of the slash 5 models, the points had been housed in a cavity at the bottom of the crankcase, beneath the advance unit, which made adjusting the timing more difficult than it had to be. Now the points were placed in a self-contained housing for simpler timing adjustment. A single-row cam chain with a master link to facilitate replacement replaced the old double-row version, and a spring-loaded, hydraulically damped cam chain tensioner was also installed to reduce chain whip. The drive shaft received a spring-loaded ramped coupler. This acted as a shock absorber and helped minimize the infamous BMW shift clunk. Finally, cast wheels became standard for all models.

Not much changed for 1980. A new air box was installed, as was a pulse air-injection system designed to minimize exhaust emissions.

A big change or two did follow in 1981, when Brembo calipers replaced the traditional ATE units that BMW had used since they began to fit disc brakes. At the same time, electronic ignition superseded the old and dated breaker point ignition. Galnikal plated cylinders replaced the old iron alloy bores, reducing cylinder wear, while a deeper oil sump lowered oil temperature slightly.

In 1984 the 1,000-cc engine was dropped and the R80 acquired a new fork, a single-sided swingarm and alloy wheels. Detail changes included a new exhaust system with megaphone looking mufflers. The styling was somewhat angular and not to everyone's taste. The bike proved to be a good performer though, with excellent road manners, and it managed to stay in production until 1994, when it was replaced by the 850R.

PROBLEMS

By and large, all of the R80 and R100 models are paragons of reliability; however, there are some things to watch for. Along with all of the other airhead twins built from 1970 up, the transmission input shaft splines need an occasional coating of antiseize compound. Along those same lines, you'll run into the odd gearbox that needs reshimming. This seems to occur more often on the R100s than any of the other bikes, but the procedure is neither complicated nor terribly expensive—although I do recommend having it done at an authorized dealer. Early R100s, much like the their /5 predecessors, also have a problem with blow-by that creates rear main seal leaks. The blow-by is caused by worn-out top ends. When the top end is past its prime, combustion gases get forced past the rings, which pressurizes the bottom end. The breather cannot evacuate the crankcase pressure fast enough, so the pressure forces its way past the rear main seal. Simply replacing the rear main seal is only a temporary fix. The real solution is a fresh top end. If the bike you're looking at has a puddle of oil beneath the rear main seal, factor in the price of a fresh top end, and a rear main seal, including labor.

Valve seat recession: This is the biggie. Toward the end of the 1970s, the EPA phased out lead as a fuel additive. In 1980 new valve seats were fitted to all models. The timing couldn't have been worse. Within a short time the valves started to tighten up, particularly the exhaust valves. The new seats had poor heat transfer characteristics, and simply weren't compatible with lead-free fuel. The under-stressed R80s suffered less than the R100s, but problems can affect all models. The first sign of trouble is a poor idle that can't be cured by adjustment or tune-up. Reduced valve clearance is a tip-off as well. In 1988 BMW released a tool steel valve seat that solved the problem. It's unusual these days to find a bike that hasn't been upgraded, but they are out there. The problem is well known and easily repaired, so don't let the specter of valve-seat recession put you off of an otherwise decent bike.

What They Said at the Time

"BMW's latest model replaces the R75/7 with more displacement, smoother shifting, a turn signal beeper, and a larger price tag. But is it any better?" *Cycle,* January 1978

"The standard (R100) T is big, powerful, smooth, and comfortable." *Cycle Street and Touring Buyer's Guide,* 1980

BMW Buyers Guide Spec Sheet—R80/7 (1977–1983), R100 (1976–1983), R100S (1976–1978)

Engine type ————————— Overhead valve, flat twin

Displacement ————————— 785 cc (R80), 980 cc (R100)

Compression ratio ————— 9.2:1 (R80 1978–1979), 9.5:1 (R100), 8.2:1 (R80 after 1980)

Ignition ————————— Battery and coil, electronic ignition (all models after 1981)

Carburetion ————————— Dual Bing 32mm CV carburetors (R80), dual Bing 34mm CV carbs (all R100)

Horsepower ————————— 55 bhp @ 7,000 rpm (R80), 70 bhp @ 7,250 rpm (all R100 models *except* 1976 R100: 60 bhp and 1976 R100S: 65 bhp)

Electrical system ————— 12 volt, alternator

Transmission ————————— 5-speed, shaft driven

Weight ————————— 430 lbs (R80, R100/7), 436 lbs (R100T), 441 lbs (R100S)

Instruments ————————— Tachometer, speedometer, neutral light, high-beam indicator, charging indicator, directional indicator, low oil pressure indicator, low brake fluid light (clock and voltmeter standard on R100T and R100S, optional on R80 and R100)

Frame ————————— Welded steel, duplex cradle

Suspension ————————— Telescopic front fork, swing arm rear, Monolever (R80, 1984 and later)

Tire size ————————— 3.25 × 19 front, 4.00 × 18 rear

0-60 ————————— n/a (R80), 4.6 seconds (R100)

Standing start 1/4 mile — 13.78 seconds (R80), 13.26 seconds (R100, R100S)

Top speed ————————— 110 mph (R80), 115 mph (R100)

Watch for seats that rub on the fuel tank on early models.

A "loud valve tick" may actually be a broken rocker arm needle bearing. If there is lots of top-end clatter, you may want to pop off a valve cover.

After 1980, valve seat recession became a problem.

Fork springs tend to sag.

The centerstand is still pretty junky.

R100RT (1979-1994)
R80RT (1982-1994)

Chapter 11
The *Gummikuh*

Introduced in late 1978 as a 1979 model bike, the full-fairing RT was BMW's first dip of the toe into the swirling full-dress-luxo-touring waters. Apparently it found it to its liking, because the RT in one form or another has become a mainstay of the BMW line-up. Mechanically the bike is little different from any of the other 1-liter twins of the day. Therefore, anything that applies to any of the standard R100s holds true for the RT, or the R80. Based loosely on the RS, the RT featured a full fairing with integral side storage compartments, an adjustable windshield, and wide bars with an upright seating position.

With a list price of $6,345, the 1979 R100RT was easily the most expensive bike generally available bike on the market. The initial version was released wearing a white seat, matching lowers, and a brownish upper fairing and fuel tank. The side covers were painted in the same off-white as the lower fairing half. Although the quality of the bike was in keeping with BMW tradition, the price was high, even when considering the many standard features. Krauser bags, a small luggage rack, and voltmeter and clock were all part of the RT package.

Overall, the RT was a good performer, if not an outstanding one. It had adequate power, it handled decently, and its brakes were OK. The weather protection was outstanding, and it did have plenty of storage space, which made it a favorite of the long-distance touring crowd. It also had the BMW roundel on the tank and the long-term reliability that the emblem stood for. Still, it was nowhere near a big seller, in part because the looks were a bit odd and in part because full-boat touring had yet to catch on—and of course there was the price, which in 1979 was high enough to give you a nose bleed.

In 1981 the RT received some substantial updates along with the rest of the BMW line, which are detailed in Chapter 10. Peculiar to the RT were a pair of Boge-Nivomat self-leveling shock absorbers. It was a clever idea, but answered a question no one was asking. The twin-shock version of the RT was dropped in 1984. After lying dormant for three years, it reappeared in 1987 with a single-sided swing arm. Or, rather a new R100RT appeared. This was basically an overboard R80RT.

Perhaps believing the old adage that less is more, BMW launched the R80RT in 1982. The spec sheet revealed a smaller engine and migration of the clock and voltmeter to the options list. In 1984 the 800 was relaunched with a single-sided swing arm. The Monolever was accompanied by a stout new front end and a fork brace. The combination must have worked well—the 800-cc version of the RT outsold its larger brother by a margin of three to one.

Overall, any of the RT series are reliable, long-lived motorcycles. Problems are few, and mostly confined to the very early models of the R100RT, which suffer from the same faults as the rest of the airheads. Valve-seat recession should be considered on the appropriate years; however, most of those bikes have long since been repaired. Many RTs will have accumulated high mileage, but you'd expect nothing else from a dedicated touring bike—and all things being equal, high mileage on a BMW is a very nebulous factor.

1989 R100RT $3995

What They Said at the Time

"The R100RT can lug your gear, keep you dry, get over 47 miles per gallon, and sing the song of the open road, all at once." *Cycle*, April 1979

"The BMW R100RT remains high on our list as a great fellow traveler." *Cycle*, March 1981

BMW Buyers Guide Spec Sheet— R100RT (1979–1994)

Engine type	Overhead valve, flat twin
Displacement	980 cc
Compression ratio	9.5:1, 8.2:1 (1980 and later)
Ignition	Battery and coil (1979–80), inductive magnetically triggered (1981 and later)
Carburetion	Dual 40mm CV Bing
Horsepower	70 bhp @ 7,250 rpm
Electrical system	12 volt, alternator
Transmission	5-speed
Weight	516 lbs
Instruments	Tachometer, speedometer, neutral light, high-beam indicator, charging indicator, directional indicator, low oil pressure, low brake fluid light, clock, and voltmeter
Frame	Welded steel, duplex cradle
Suspension	Telescopic front fork, rear swing arm with Nivomat self-leveling shock absorbers (later models with monolever rear suspension)
Tire size	3.25 × 19 front, 4.00 × 18 rear
0-60	n/a
Standing start 1/4 mile:	13.5 seconds (1981)
Top speed	127 mph (calculated)

BMW Buyer's Guide Spec Sheet—R80RT 1982 (twin shock), 1984–1994 (Monolever)

Engine type	Overhead valve, flat twin
Displacement	798 cc
Compression ratio	8.2:1
Ignition	Bosch electronic
Carburetion	Dual 32mm CV Bing Carburetors
Horsepower	50 bhp @ 6,500 rpm
Electrical system	12 volt, alternator
Transmission	5-speed
Weight	472 lbs (twin shock), 463 lbs (Monolever)
Instruments	Tachometer, speedometer, neutral light, high-beam indicator, charging indicator, directional indicator, low oil pressure light, low brake fluid light, clock, and voltmeter
Frame	Welded steel, duplex cradle
Suspension	Telescopic front fork and rear swing arm, Monolever rear arm (1984 and later)
Tire size	100/90 × 19 front, 120/90 × 18 rear (1982–1983); 90/90 × 18 front, 120/90 × 18 rear (1984–1994)
0-60	5.9 seconds
Standing start 1/4 mile	13.9 seconds
Top speed	115 mph (calculated)

Windshields become crazed over—look to the aftermarket for a decent replacement.

R80RTs suffer from the occasional charging fault. BMW introduced an upgraded wiring harness that provides a better ground for the diode board, which does help.

Early R100RTs have all the faults of the /7 line.

If the Nivomats shocks are kaput, consider a contemporary replacement.

R65, R65LS (1979-1984)

Big Frame Version (1985-1993)

Chapter 12
Small and Sweet

Toward the end of 1970s, BMW found itself without any sort of midsize motorcycle, so it did the logical thing and built one. The R65 had its roots firmly stuck in Europe, where it was used as a base model to create a small, entry-level bike, the R45, and to sneak under an insurance guideline increasing the premium on bikes over 700 cc. BMW could have simply downsized the existing R80, as it did to create the R50 from the R75, but to its credit it didn't. The R65 got its own short-stroke engine and its own frame and running gear.

The R65 was a delightful little bike that was released to the U.S. market just in time for the 1979 selling season. Most of the parts for the R65 were purpose-built, rather than shared, and the bike is much better for it. The R65 was one of the few BMWs that could be termed nimble. While the very first of the R65s were a wee bit reluctant to start when the temperature dropped below 50 degrees or so, this was quickly traced to EPA jetting. Raising the needle a clip for the first few hundred miles solved the problem. If there was any inherent problem, it was only that the bike itself was a little small for riders approaching the 6-foot mark. The bike could also be a bit buzzy at the federally mandated 55-mile-per-hour speed limit; however, at 60 and up it was smooth as glass. The R65 at 45 horsepower was also a bit down on power, particularly for the American market. So in 1981 larger intake valves were installed to boost output

to 50 horsepower—an improvement, although still a bit tame for U.S. tastes.

Nonetheless, the bike could give a very good account of itself on winding back roads. Brakes were very good and had a particularly good feel to them. The suspension was typical of any BMW motorcycle from this period—lots of lightly damped travel. Most bikes of the same period had less travel and much heavier damping. The ride was comfortable, and the bike maintained its composure right up to the point where the hard parts dragged. Overall, a very nice motorcycle and one seldom seen today. Due to its small size, the R65 really isn't for everyone, especially if long-distance touring is your forte. However, if you fit the bike, or simply prefer a small motorcycle, the R65 may be just your cup of chowder.

In 1981 BMW decided the R65 needed a sportier image, so it turned noted designer Hans Muth loose again. The result was a sharply styled "pocket rocket" called the LS. The LS differed from the standard version in several respects. Most notably, it had a small quarter-fairing that housed the instruments. It also had twin front disc brakes, white mags that used a slightly different spoke pattern than the standard R65, and a blacked-out exhaust system. There were other styling cues, like black mirrors and black handlebars all set off by bright paintwork. The seat had a pair of handholds built into it, and it was of a slightly different shape than the standards. Overall, the bike had a sharp look to it, much like the Suzuki Katana, another Muth job. The LS never sold particularly well, so there are few of them about; however, it's a very nice collectible today and a lot of fun to ride.

"BIG FRAME" VERSION

Starting with the 1985 model line, the LS version was discontinued and the R65 engine was dropped into standard R80 cycle parts. At the same time, the engine was retuned to provide more low-end grunt by reducing the compression from 9.2:1 to 8.7:1. The bike was still a decent performer, and it was the cheapest bike in the BMW line-up. But the reality was that it wasn't *that* much cheaper than the R80. The bike was never very popular, particularly in the U.S. market. As an inexpensive working classic, and I use the term loosely, it wouldn't be a bad buy, but in all other respects I'd prefer the earlier version.

Few problems are endemic to the R65. In large part they are among the best BMWs ever built. They are easy to work on, suffer none of the engine problems of their larger brethren, and tend to be easy on clutches and transmissions. I'd avoid the later, large-frame versions, but that may be my prejudices creeping in. Functionally there is little wrong with them.

What They Said at the Time

BMW Buyer's Guide Spec Sheet—R65–R65 LS (1979–1984), R65 Monolever (1985–1993)

Engine type	Overhead valve, flat twin
Displacement	650 cc
Compression ratio	9.2:1 (1979–1983), 8.7:1 (1984–1993)
Ignition	Battery and coil (1979–1980), Bosch electronic (1981 and later)
Carburetion	Dual 32mm Bing CV Carburetors
Horsepower	45 bhp @ 7,250 rpm (1979–1980), 50 bhp (1981–1983); 48 bhp @ 7,250 rpm (1984–1993)
Electrical system	12 volt alternator
Transmission	5-speed
Weight	438 lbs (R65), 451 lbs (R65LS), 461 lbs (Monolever)
Instruments	Speedometer, tachometer, neutral light, high-beam indicator, charging indicator, directional indicator, low oil pressure light
Frame	Welded steel, duplex cradle
Suspension	Telescopic front fork, rear swing arm, Monolever (1984 and later)
Tire size	100/90 × 18 front, 120/90 × 18 rear (R65/R65LS); 90/90 × 18 front, 120/90 × 18 rear (1984)
0-60	5.5 seconds (1981 LS), n/a (R65)
Standing start 1/4 mile	14.09 seconds (1979 R65), 13.99 seconds (1981 R65LS)
Top speed	112 mph (1979 R65, calculated), 101 mph (1981 R65 LS, actual)

Some of the early bikes (built in late 1978–early 1979) suffered from soft valves. In extreme cases, the valve head could be yanked off the stem. Normally this only occurred on bikes with over 40,000 miles. Obviously, if you stumble on an early R65 with an unknown history, it might be a wise move to pull the heads and take a good look at the valves with an eye toward replacing them. The valves were redesigned at the beginning of 1980 and no further problems arose.

Very early bikes had some main bearing issues. The front main bearing was slightly oversized. This allowed oil pressure to drop, and after about 30,000 miles the oil pump would grind its way into the crankcase—not a very good situation. Presumably these bikes have either been repaired or they've blown up and gone away.

Diode boards and rotors are known to fail, though it's not a widespread problem.

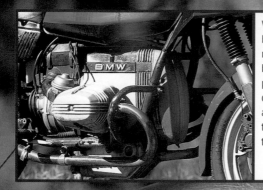

Valve guide wear can be a problem on high mileage bikes. If the bike smokes heavily, particularly on a closed throttle, figure a set of guides into the cost of a routine top end overhaul.

Some of the mag wheels tend to be a wee bit soft, especially on early bikes. Check them carefully for any dings, dents, or cracks, especially up front.

Airhead G/S and GS (1980-1995), R80ST (1982-1984)

Chapter 13
Getting Dirty

G/S

When the G/S was introduced to the world motorcycle press in the fall of 1980, no one quite knew what to make of it. Of course, old hands recalled BMW's long and proud history in the ISDT (International Six-Day Trial, the precursor to today's International Six-Day Enduro) and smiled knowingly as did those graybeards who waxed on nostalgically over the old desert sleds like the Triumph TR6C and Norton PII. But in general the motorcycling public, specifically those who thought of BMW as a touring, or at best a sport/touring, brand were perplexed, to say the least. At a time when a 500-cc single cylinder off-road bike was considered huge, the twin cylinder, 800-cc BMW was an absolute dreadnought. Well, yes and no. Although the "G" stands for Gelande or off-road and the "S" for Strasse or street/road, the GS was never really intended to be a giant enduro bike. What it was intended to be, and what it ultimately became, was the forerunner of a new type of motorcycle—the adventure bike. Suffice to say that the GS not only sired this new breed, but in all honesty has remained at the absolute head of the class from day one.

The concept of the GS began with the R75/5 ISDT bikes. These were the genuine article and won more than their share of grueling off-road events. Around 1975 several BMW engineers built ISDT replicas for their own use, and these created quite a stir around the factory. In 1979, upper management decided that such a bike had some sales merit and gave the go-ahead for the bike that became known as the R80G/S.

After a short development period, the G/S hit U.S. showrooms in late 1980, just in time for the 1981 selling season.

The R80G/S bore some resemblance to the street model, but not much. The front wheel was replaced with a 21-inch version. The front fender was a high-mounted off-road model made of plastic. The exhaust used a two-into-one configuration that ran along the left side, terminating in a large muffler. Most notably, the G/S featured the first single-sided swing arm, the Monolever. The bike was finished in bright white with blue and red Motorsport decals on the flanks of the fuel tank. The seat was a bright lobster red, somewhat gaudy, but in keeping with the bike's character. There was also a somewhat staid, blue version available for the more conservative adventurer. The instrument console held only a speedometer and some warning lights. A tachometer was available as an option, though, and was often added at the dealership. Like all of the BMW range of that year, the G/S got the full engine update package, Bosch electronic ignition, redesigned oiling, and a deeper sump.

In 1981, Hubert Auriol won the Paris-Dakar rally aboard a modified R80G/S, the first of many wins for BMW. The bike also began to become the choice of the hardcore traveler. Hardcore in this instance meaning borderline nutcases who thought a short trip for coffee meant riding to Columbia and having a cup with Juan Valdez, preferably in 48 hours or less.

In 1984, BMW decided to commemorate its success in the desert by launching the Paris-Dakar version of the R80. The P/D version included a 7-gallon fuel tank, Paris/Dakar graphics, and a solo seat. There was also a kit available to retrofit these parts to standard models.

The second generation of the GS—the slash was now deleted—was released in 1988. Although there were both 800- and 1,000-cc versions, only the 1,000-cc R100GS was available in the United States. Everything, save the blue and white emblem on the tank, was new and genuinely better. Up front was a Marzocchi fork: Never again would the GS nose dive like a pole-axed mule when the front brakes were applied. The front wheel, still a 21-inch, now had the spokes running from the hub to the periphery of the rim, as did the 17-inch rear wheel. This permitted the use of tubeless tires on spoked rims. The Monolever rear swingarm was gone, replaced by a Paralever. The engine now displaced a full 1,000 cc and made 60 horsepower, as compared to the R80's 50. Standard equipment included crash bars and a luggage rack, as well as an engine oil cooler. In addition to the much-improved standard seat, an optional taller seat was available. An upgraded starter, lighter and stronger, was also installed. As a bonus, a higher-capacity battery was now used.

PARIS-DAKAR (R100GS PARIS-DAKAR)

Starting with the 1990 model year, BMW decided a 1,000-cc version of the Paris-Dakar was in order. If the PD looked a bit ostentatious, it was intentional. The bike looked as much like a piece of light ordnance as it did a motorcycle. For starters, the headlight/number plate of the standard GS was replaced with a neat fairing that flowed into the extra large 8.7-gallon fuel tank. Crash-bars protected the engine, the fairing, and presumably the rider. There was a large skid plate, solo seat, and extended luggage rack. Saddlebag mounts were included, although the bags themselves were an option. If you wanted to roll your own, all of the parts required to create a PD version were available through your local dealer.

R80ST

The R80ST released in 1982 was essentially an 800-cc GS that was set up as a pure street bike. The front fork was replaced with one that was similar to the one on the R65, as was the frame. The wheels were conventional 19-inch front and 18-inch rear. The Monolever rear swing arm was used, as was

the two-into-one exhaust pipe. Overall, the bike was lithe, light, and fun to ride. Unfortunately, it didn't sell very well and was dropped at the end of 1984.

What They Said at the Time

"Adventurers and explorers will immediately see the value of the of G/S." *Cycle*, December 1980

"All we know is that the bike is wild, wonderful, and a little bit wicked. And we know we love it." *Cycle World*, December 1989

"What you get for your money is a light, agile, uncomplicated, clean, attractive motorcycle." *Cycle World*, October 1983

Trouble Spots

These bikes were all damn reliable; however, Paralever bikes do suffer from some rear bearing wear, so make sure you check it.

MONOLEVER VS. PARALEVER

To put it simply, the Monolever is nothing more than a conventional swing arm with one side removed. While single-sided swing arms have become more popular in recent years, BMW was the first major manufacturer bold enough to actually offer a bike so equipped to the general public. Engineers reasoned that because the right side of the swing arm had to contain the drive shaft, it was robust enough, with some modification, to support the rear wheel on its own. Experiments proved this true, so BMW decided to test the waters by offering the Monolever, as it became known, on the 1980 R80GS. As a side issue, BMW felt that the GS was a quirky bike in its own right and that the typical owner wouldn't be put off by the odd looks of the single-sided swing arm. In addition, it offered several advantages over the conventional design—it was somewhat cheaper to build and it facilitated quick tire changes. In all other respects, the Monolever works exactly like a traditional, double-sided swing arm.

On the other hand, the Paralever actually solves a problem that has plagued shaft-driven bikes ever since the adoption of the swinging-arm rear suspension. The problem is that drive forces conveyed to the rear wheel through the drive shaft upset chassis behavior: under acceleration the bike tends to lift; during deceleration it tends to squat. This is known as "jacking." Longtime BMW riders simply got used to the phenomenon. The problem was that as the engines became more powerful, jacking became a real issue, and BMW wanted to eliminate as much of it as possible.

The easiest way to eliminate jacking is to fit stiff rear springs or to extend the swing arm. BMW didn't want stiffer rear suspension. And achieving the desired effect the other way would have required a swing arm longer than the bike itself. What it needed was a way to make a normal-length swing arm behave as if it was twice as long.

The solution was to install a second U-joint in the drive shaft just forward of the final drive. The rear drive housing was then redesigned so that it was free to pivot in the swing-arm tube. A strut was installed from the bottom of the rear drive to the transmission. The rear shock was bolted to the top of the drive and to the frame. The end result of all this jiggery-pokery is a modified parallelogram-style swing arm, hence the name Paralever. Because a parallelogram feeds the majority of the reaction forces back into the frame, it can be built to the same length as a conventional swing arm, yet it effectively cancels out 70 percent of the jacking effect. What's left is so small as to be completely negligible.

All Airhead GS models R80GS (1980–1987), R100GS (1988–1994) Paris Dakar and Mystic

BMW Buyer's Guide Spec Sheet—R80GS–R80PD

Engine type	Overhead valve, flat twin
Displacement	797 cc
Compression ratio	8.2:1
Ignition	Bosch electronic
Carburetion	Dual 32mm Bing CV carburetors
Horsepower	50 bhp @ 6,500 rpm
Electrical system	12 volt, alternator
Transmission	5-speed, shaft driven
Weight	421 lbs
Instruments	Speedometer, turn signal indicators, high-beam indicator, neutral light, charge, and low oil pressure indicators
Frame	Welded steel, duplex cradle
Suspension	Telescopic front fork, single-sided Monolever swing arm
Tire size	3.00 × 21 front, 4.00 × 18 rear
0-60	5.5 seconds
Standing start 1/4 mile	13.81 seconds
Top speed	105 mph, although the official top speed was listed at a maximum of 93 mph due to the off-road tires used

BMW Buyer's Guide Spec Sheet—R100GS–R100PD (1988–1994)

Engine type	Overhead valve, flat twin
Displacement	980 cc
Compression ratio	8.5:1
Ignition	Bosch electronic
Carburetion	Dual 32mm Bing CV Carburetors
Horsepower	58 bhp @ 6,500 rpm
Electrical system	12 volt, alternator
Transmission	5-speed, shaft driven
Weight	463 lbs, 485 lbs (P/D version with large tank)
Instruments	Speedometer, neutral, high-beam and turn signal indicators, warning lights for low battery, low oil pressure
Frame	Welded steel, duplex cradle
Suspension	Telescopic front fork (Marzocchi), Paralever rear swing arm
Tire size	90/90 × 21 front, 130/80 × 17 rear
0-60	4.7 seconds
Standing start 1/4 mile	13.74 seconds
Top speed	102 mph (measured)

BMW Buyer's Guide Spec Sheet—R80ST (1982–1984)

Engine type	Overhead valve, flat twin
Displacement	797 cc
Compression ratio	8.2:1
Ignition	Bosch electronic
Carburetion	Dual 32mm CV Bing Carburetors
Horsepower	50 bhp @ 6,500 rpm
Electrical system	12 volt, alternator
Transmission	5-speed, shaft driven
Weight	403.5 lbs
Instruments	Speedometer, tachometer, low oil pressure warning light, low battery warning light, turn signal, high-beam indicator lights
Frame	Welded steel, double cradle
Suspension	Telescopic front fork, Monolever swing arm
Tire size	100/90 × 19 front, 120/90 × 18 rear
0-60	5.6 seconds
Standing start 1/4 mile	13.81 seconds
Top speed	105 mph (measured)

As with all Airheads, valve seat recession can be a problem, particularly on early 1,000-cc versions.

The rear bearing on Paralever swingarms is prone to wearing out. You will have to replace it at roughly 30,000-mile intervals.

The transmission input shaft should be lubricated every two years or so.

Crash bar-mounted oil coolers are prone to crash damage. If the oil cooler looks a little tweaked, take a close look at the mounts and make sure they haven't cracked.

Rotors and diode boards are known to fail periodically.

R100CS, R100R, Mystic, R100RS

Chapter 14
The Last and Best of the Airheads

R100CS (1981–1984)

By rights the CS could easily fit in a previous chapter. Be that as it may, since it was the last of the airheads in the S range, it ended up here. The R100CS is arguably the most sophisticated of the S range. It was sold with the abbreviated fairing and S-style dual seat with attached luggage rack. Mechanically, the CS was identical to the rest of the 1,000-cc line-up.

R100R (1991–1994)

The R100R was the last gasp for the airhead twin. Conceived as a back-to-basics roadster, hence the R, the bike was available in two versions. The first was exactly what it purported to be—a simple and straight-forward BMW. The 1,000-cc motor was fitted with 42-millimeter carburetors; compression was a modest 8.5:1. An oil cooler was hung just below the steering head. The silver-painted frame utilized the Paralever-type swing arm, and had a Showa rear shock that was preload adjustable and fitted with adjustable rebound damping. The front fork was also a Showa unit. Up front, a single Brembo caliper provided the brakes, while a drum controlled the rear. Reinforcing the classic theme were wire wheels with through-the-rim spokes, which allowed the use of tubeless tires. The seat had an odd two-tone finish, but it was comfortable. Rounded valve covers completed the historic-theme look.

For some bizarre reason, BMW also offered a "custom version" complete with added chrome, psychedelic paint and the word BOXER emblazoned on the tank, just in case you weren't sure, I suppose. Not a whole lot of these were sold, and if you run across one you'll understand why.

R100R MYSTIC (1994)

The Mystic was a one-year-only modification to the basic 100R. The bike was finished in a very attractive Mystic red metallic paint scheme, hence the name. The rest of the styling cues were also unique. The seat and tail section were totally redesigned and gave the bike the swoopy good looks of a dedicated superbike. Low, flat, sport-type handlebars and a redesigned instrument cluster continued the theme. The exhaust system was tucked in to provide better ground clearance and a sportier look. Dual front disc brakes were utilized although the rear stopper was still a drum.

R100RS

In 1984, BMW announced the end of the 1,000-cc twins. Out of the good graces of its corporate heart, BMW was going to make 250RS and RT "Last Edition" versions available to anyone with the desire and the cash. These bikes were painted pearl white and given the appropriate commemorative decals; presumably there wasn't a dry eye in the house as an RS rolled off the assembly line for the last time. At least until 1988, when BMW decided that you can never have too much of a good thing and released the Monolever version of the 1,000-cc RS and RT. As you may imagine, this didn't sit well with owners of "Last Edition" models, who now seemed to have second-to-last edition bikes. The Monolever bike was attractive enough, notwithstanding the fact that the solo seat was no longer an option. Potential buyers were also a bit surprised that BMW chose the Monolever rear suspension over the latest generation Paralever used on the GS. The other big surprise was that the new RS was considerably detuned. Carburetor size was reduced from 40 millimeters to 32 millimeters. The inlet valve size was also reduced from the original 44 millimeters to 42, although the exhaust valve remained at 40. The cam was somewhat softer and the new exhaust also robbed a few horsepower. The compression ratio was bumped up slightly, from 8.2:1 to 8.5:1, so the new bike wouldn't be an absolute pooch. Overall the changes were good for a loss of 12 horsepower, although bottom-end torque was somewhat improved—the new version making 55 lb-ft at 3,500 rpm, compared to the 55.7 lb-ft at 5,500 rpm of the early models.

Despite the vasectomy, the new RS was just as fast as the old version, if not slightly faster, at least up to the ton mark. This was due to the Monolver bike being slightly lighter, and having its torque curve a lot fatter down low, which enabled the rider to get the bike out of the gate a lot quicker. It also kept the bike in the fat part of the torque curve at the speeds riders used most often. The new bike also had a new frame to go with the Monolever rear swingarm. The wheelbase was shortened by a half-inch, the rake was reduced to 27.8 degrees, and the trail increased to 4.7 inches. The 19-inch front wheel was exchanged for a slightly wider 18-inch version. The overall result was a bike that was a bit nimbler and just as stable to ride. Front brakes were a pair of 285-millimeter rotors gripped by twin-piston Brembo calipers. In fact, both the wheels and brakes were lifted from the K bikes. Unfortunately, the rear brake, which had been a disc on the previous twin-shock model, was now a lowly drum—no doubt a cost-cutting move, but strangely out of place on what was arguably BMW's flagship

twin. To add insult to injury, the new RS now carried less fuel. When the bike was redesigned, some of the electrical components previously housed in the headlight were moved to the frame backbone. This meant that the tank had to be notched to make room for them. The new tank, although externally identical to the old one, now held a gallon less, meaning that the former king of Sport Touring went on reserve at around 175 miles. Hell, the average BMW RS rider needed at least 200 miles just to work up an appetite.

VARIATIONS ON A THEME
R100R
From March 1992, BMW offered a special chrome kit that upgraded (if that's the word) the appearance of the classically styled R100R.

The chrome kit included:
    Fork brace
    Crash bar
    Valve covers
    Upper carburetor
    Rear grab handle
    Fuel tank cap
    Rear view mirrors
    Exhaust collar nut
    Instrument panel
    Turn signal housings
    Handle bar-end weights

Further Variations:
    The Mystic (1994 only)
    Mystic red metallic paint
    Chrome headlight mount
    Chrome instrument cover
    Chrome-plated turn signal supports
    Low, sport-type handlebar
    Revised seat and tail section
    New black-painted rear subframe
    New battery covers
    Abbreviated license plate support
    Tucked-in muffler

What They Said at the Time

"Almost without realizing it, you come to understand how the same basic design can survive for 68 years." *Cycle World*, March 1992

"[The R100RS is] great for riders who appreciate virtues that gain luster with age." *Cycle*, July 1988

R100R, R100R Mystic (1991–1995), R100CS (1980–1984), R100RS (1986–1992)

BMW Buyer's Guide Spec Sheet— R100R/Mystic (1991–1995)

Engine type	Overhead valve, flat twin
Displacement	980 cc
Compression ratio	8.5:1
Ignition	Bosch electronic
Carburetion	Dual 32mm Bing carburetors
Horsepower	48.5 bhp @ 6,500 rpm
Electrical system	12 volt, alternator
Transmission	5-speed, shaft driven
Weight	435 lbs
Instruments	Speedometer, tachometer, warning lights for low oil pressure and charge, indicators for high-beam and turn signals
Frame	Welded steel, double cradle
Suspension	Telescopic front fork, Paralver swing arm
Tire size	110/80 × 18 front, 140/80 × 17 rear
0-60	4.6 seconds
Standing start 1/4 mile	13.27 seconds
Top speed	109 mph

BMW Buyer's Guide Spec Sheet— R100CS (1980–1984)

Engine type ————— Overhead valve, flat twin
Displacement ——— 980 cc
Compression ratio ——— 8.2:1
Ignition ————— Bosch electronic
Carburetion ————— Dual 40mm Bing CV carburetors
Horsepower ————— 70 bhp @ 7,000 rpm
Electrical system ——— 12 volt, alternator
Transmission ——— 5-speed, shaft driven
Weight ————— 441 lbs
Instruments ——— Speedometer, tachometer, volt meter, clock, low oil pressure warning light, charging indicator light, turn signal and high-beam indicator
Frame ————— Welded steel, double cradle
Suspension ————— Telescopic front, swing arm rear
Tire size ————— 3.25 × 19 front, 4.00 × 18 rear
0-60 ————— 5.3 seconds
Standing start 1/4 mile — 13.18 seconds
Top speed ————— 114 mph

BMW Buyer's Guide Spec Sheet— R100RS–Monolever (1986–1992)

Engine type ————— Overhead valve, flat twin
Displacement ——— 980 cc
Compression ratio ——— 8.5:1
Ignition ————— Bosch electronic
Carburetion ————— Dual 32mm Bing CV carburetors
Horsepower ————— 58 bhp @ 6,500 rpm
Electrical system ——— 12 volt, alternator
Transmission ——— 5-speed, shaft driven
Weight ————— 463 lbs
Instruments ——— Speedometer, tachometer, volt meter, clock, low oil pressure warning light, charging indicator light, turn signal and high-beam indicator
Frame ————— Welded steel, double cradle
Suspension ————— Telescopic front fork, Monolever rear swing arm
Tire size ————— 90/90 × 18 front, 120/90 × 18 rear
0-60 ————— n/a
Standing start 1/4 mile — 13.3 seconds
Top speed ————— 115 mph

R100RS: Rear shock gives up the ghost quite quickly. Aftermarket replacements add value; consider the cost of a new shock if the bike still has the original Showa.

R100R: Watch that Paralever rear bearing, especially on bikes with over 30,000 miles.

In general, the last airhead BMWs were notoriously trouble free.

The single-row cam chain used from 1979 on tends to wear out between 25,000 and 30,000 miles. The bikes will run nearly forever with a worn chain, but they can be noisy. The noise mimics a loose valve, so this can be tricky to diagnose.

Oilheads 2000 All Models

Chapter 15

The Boxer Reborn

It's time to shift gears. With rare exception, all of the BMWs profiled thus far have some value as collectibles or at least as working classics. This is an arguable point of course, but in the main it's true. The R259 engine-bikes, or oilheads, as most call them, are too new to be considered anything but modern motorcycles. Whether they will become collectible motorcycles is debatable; what they are now, as far as this book is concerned, are high-end previously owned and somewhat quirky motorcycles.

The first of the new generation, R259 boxer-motored bikes made their appearance late in 1993 as 1994 models. Essentially they share nothing save basic design philosophy with any of the bikes that went before them. True, they are shaft-driven boxer twins with a well-earned reputation for reliability. But there the similarity ends. As you'll see, they owe as much to the design of the legendary Vincent motorcycle as they do to anything from Munich.

ENGINE DESIGN

The R259 motor began life as an 1,100-cc model; later variations included 1,150-, 850- and 1,200-cc versions.

The engine features a vertically split crankcase with the oil sump cast in unit, the sump holding 4.5 liters (1 gallon). The halves are sealed with a silicone compound. The 1,100-cc.motor has a high 10.7:1 compression ratio; other engines vary slightly but all run some where close to 10:1 or better, requiring the use of premium fuel.

The crankshaft uses two main bearings; the inclusion of a third (center) bearing would increase the distance between the connecting rods, which would accentuate any rocking couple between the con-rods, increasing vibration.

The rods are created from powdered/sintered metal. They are forged as one piece and then the big ends fractured. This creates an incredibly strong, very light rod with a self-aligning main bearing cap.

Pistons are exceptionally light, with only a wisp of a skirt. Three rings are used: one for oil control, and two to seal the top end. The cylinders are finished with Gilnisil, a low-friction, nickel-silicone coating.

Four-valve heads are employed on all models. The problem was how to open them. Overhead cams would have made the engine objectionably tall, and ground clearance would have suffered. The solution was to have the crankshaft drive a jackshaft, located beneath it, at half engine speed. Chains then transfer the motion to camshafts located at the bottom of each head. Short pushrods transfer the cam action to forked rocker arms, which open the valves.

Fuel delivery is by Bosch Motronic injection, and exhaust emissions are controlled via a three-way catalytic converter.

Dependent on the model, the transmission is either fitted with five or six speeds, driving, of course, through a shaft.

Although BMW considered water-cooling, it would have increased weight, and complexity. Accordingly a combination of air and oil cooling was chosen. The oil pump pushes the oil through a series of drilled passages that circulate over, under, and around all the hot spots. The oil is routed around the exhaust valve seats to prevent localized overheating. Since shutting off a hot engine could cause any residual oil left in the passages to overheat and form carbon, particularly in the exhaust valve region, stand pipes were inserted to hold enough oil to absorb the heat, preventing the formation of coke or carbon. Oil radiators are provided to manage the oil temperature.

FRAME

There is no frame as such. A light grillwork mounts the seat, the tank, and any components that may need mounting, such as the fairing on the RS model. The front suspension—calling it a fork doesn't do it justice—mounts to a superstructure bolted to the top of the engine. In the rear, a Paralever fulfills the role of swing arm. The top of the shock mounts to the subframe.

Up front, suspension action is controlled by BMW's unique Telelever front fork. Two fork sliders, similar to those used on standard forks, carry the front wheel. Above the front wheel is a fork brace that ties the two sliders together.

Mounted in the center of the fork brace is a ball joint. The stud of the ball joint connects it to an A-frame-style lower control arm. The legs of the control arm are mounted to the engine crankcase. At the top of the fork is another bridge, much like a conventional top clamp. A second ball joint connects this brace to the superstructure bolted onto the engine. Damping and springing is provided by a coilover hydraulic damper unit that mounts between the lower A-arm and the "frame." The Telelever fork is much more rigid than a conventional telescopic, and is less maintenance intensive. It also provides some built-in antidive characteristics.

Since the performance envelope had been greatly

expanded, BMW felt it wise to upgrade the brakes. Brembo four-piston calipers were used with 12.2-inch discs (RS version) and a single 11.4-inch disc with a two-piston Brembo caliper went out back (RS version). ABS was offered as an option the first year and became standard on later models.

BY THE NUMBERS

R1100RS–1994

The R1100RS was the first of the oilheads released. Two versions were available—one with a full fairing, one with an abbreviated version. ABS was an option, and 85 percent of the bikes delivered to the United States had it installed. To accommodate a wider range of riders, the angle of the handlebars was adjustable, and they could be moved forward and backward by about 1 inch. the seat featured a three-position adjustment as well: the total difference in height from the lowest position to the highest was again about 1 inch. In general, the RS makes a fine sport tourer, perhaps with the emphasis more on touring than sheer sport. Nonetheless, the RS holds its own on Sunday morning sport rides. Early bikes had more than their share of transmission rattles, mainly with the bike in neutral with the clutch disengaged. BMW modified the gearbox to reduce the noise. This was done as a running change though, so early production 1994 models do rattle. The rubber-mounted handlebars can be bothersome as well, but new bushings are cheap.

R1100GS–1995

The GS released in 1995 was the second oilhead out of the gate. In keeping with its off-road pretensions, the GS was slightly detuned making it a bit more tractable, especially at low speed. Like all of the new bikes, the GS came with Paralever rear and Telelever front suspension units. The Telever was reconfigured for off-road use, the travel being increased to 7.5 inches, or roughly 3 inches more than the RSs. The old 21-inch front wheel was replaced with a 19-inch. The smaller front wheel limited tire choices, but provided surer grip on the pavement, which was where 99 percent of the GSs spent 99 percent of their time. ABS was an option and 90 percent of the bikes were ordered with it. By 1998, ABS would become a standard item (a switch is installed allowing the rider to disable the ABS for off-road use.) For 2000, the GS got a facelift, a 6-speed transmission and a 1,150-cc version of the R259 engine. Because the transmission was now some-

what longer, the Paralever had to be shortened to retain the original wheelbase. Since the 2000 version was getting a new tranny case anyway, the case itself was beefed up, strengthening swing-arm pivot area.

R1100R–1995

The R model is very much a back-to-basics motorcycle. At introduction, even the tachometer was an option. The original idea was that the R would be a "roll your own" type of deal, wherein you could add whatever options you saw fit. The engine was in the same state of tune as the GS, so performance is sparkling, if not exactly incandescent. The bike is a decent performer, though, and makes an excellent "I can only afford one bike" all arounder.

R1100RT–1996

If the new RS blurred the line between sport and touring, the oilhead RT practically erased it. The RT is basically a dressed RS with a full complement of touring amenities, including an electrically adjustable windshield, and an upright seating position. The sound system is standard, as are the heated grips and saddle bags.

R1100S–1999

The blurb on the October 1998 cover of *Cycle World* summed it all up: "Is this the world's best Sport-Twin?" The R1100S is a true sport-bike, albeit one with the hard edges ground off. It makes about 10 percent more horsepower then the RS, is 22 pounds lighter than an RS (non-ABS version), and has upgraded suspension. Unlike the other oilheads, the S has its Paralever pivoting on an aluminum rear subframe rather than through the engine/transmission.

R850R–1995

Last and, unfortunately, least desirable of the oilheads, the 850s are rather scarce. Ironically, the 850R wasn't a bad bike; it just wasn't overly popular. Part of the problem was that while it was three grand cheaper than the base 1100R, when you're spending $10,000, which is about what the 850 cost headed out the door, another 3G's ain't much. Furthermore, while the 850 is certainly able to keep up with traffic, its performance does leave something to be desired. That said, the 850 is versatile, reliable, and economical to own, and lots of fun to ride, which are hard qualities to beat.

Since day one, the fuel-injected R259 engines have had a glitch in their fuel injection innards. The general complaint is that under light-to-moderate throttle, the bike bucks, spits, and snorts like an ornery mule. This is universally referred to as "surging." The lean running condition varies from bike to bike. Sometimes it's barely noticeable; at other times it's horrid. The problem is that the Bosch Motronic Engine Control Unit operates in two modes, or loops: open and closed. In open loop, the fuel data is delivered via a preprogrammed map. Open loop typically occurs during high-load situations; for example, during wide-open throttle Banzai runs. The closed-loop mode occurs during less strenuous activity, such as light acceleration and cruising. During closed-loop operation, the oxygen sensor determines fuel needs. The problem is that BMW's closed-loop programming is just too freaking lean, and the end result is a lean surge, similar to the one you'd get if the needles in a carburetor-equipped bike were set too low. Normally you'll feel the surge by popping the bike into third gear and motoring along at between 35 and 45 miles per hour.

Owners and dealers have been pounding on these bikes for 10 years now trying to get them right. They've changed plugs, cut the Cat Code Plug—which makes the bike run rich in the closed loop, but may ruin the catalytic converter—and howled at the moon. The last solution has proved as fruitful as the first two.

The only thing that I've seen that works is an aftermarket fuel-management computer—the Techlusion Fuel Nanny, 83I Powerbox, or the new Techlusion R259, for example. There are other ones out there that also work well and I offer the above only as an example. If the bike you're looking at has one of the aforementioned installed, consider it a bonus. If it doesn't, and a road test confirms that the bike does in fact surge, and it annoys you, figure $250 or so into the price for an update.

What They Said at the Time

"BMW's new R1100RS, it wouldn't be too hard to argue, is the most advanced street bike ever made." *Cycle World*, May 1993

The R1100GS "is one exceptional motorcycle, a decidedly unstandard Standard, the best of 1994." *Cycle World*, October 1994

"Finish the cars, get liquored up, and start on the bikes." *Cycle World*, June 1995 (Commenting on the 1100R's quirky styling. Overall they liked the bike a lot, though.)

"[The R1100 RT is a] great long haul tourer we'd take anywhere." *Motorcyclist*, July 2000

"Munich created in the R1100S a sporting motorcycle that holds its own in any crowd, but still plays best by BMW rules." *Motorcyclist*, December 1998

BMW Buyer's Guide Spec Sheet—Oilheads all models (1993–2000)

Engine type ———————— Overhead valve, air/oil cooled, flat twin, 4 valve, cam-in-head design

Displacement ———————— 848 cc (R850), 1,085 cc (R1100), 1,130 cc (R1150GS)

Compression ratio ———— 10.3:1 (R850, R1100, GS), 10.7:1 (R1100RS/RT)

Ignition ———————————— Bosch Motronic

Carburetion ————————— Fuel injection

Horsepower ——————————— 70 bhp @ 7,000 rpm (R850R), 80 bhp @ 6,750 rpm (R1100R, R1100GS), 90 bhp @ 7,250 rpm (R1100RS, RT), 87.3 bhp @ 7,640 rpm (R1100S—dyno tested)

Electrical system ———— 12 volt alternator (700W)

Transmission ————————— 5-speed (all except R1100S), 6-speed (R1100S, 2000 R1100GS)

Weight ——————————————— 518 lbs (R850R, R1100R), 535 lbs (R1100RS, R1100GS), 621 lbs (R1100RT), 517 lbs (R1100S)

Instruments —————————— Speedometer, tachometer, clock, warning lights for neutral, high-beam, low oil pressure, low fuel, ABS malfunction

Frame ———————————————— n/a (see chapter text)

Suspension ——————————— Telelever front, Paralever rear

Tire size ——————————— 120/70 × 17 front, 160/60 × 18 rear (R1100R, R1100RT, R1100RS); 120/70 × 17 front, 120/60 × 17 rear (R1100S); 110/80 × 19 front, 150/70 × 17 rear (R1100GS, R1150GS)

0-60 ————————————————— 3.6 seconds (R1100R), 3.5 seconds (R1100RS R1100S), 3.6 seconds (R1100GS, R1150GS), n/a (R850, R1100RT)

Standing start 1/4 mile — 12.03 seconds (R1100R), 12.21 seconds (R1100GS), 12.56 seconds (R1150GS), 12.46 seconds (R1100RT), 11.94 seconds (R1100S)

Top speed ———————————— 123 mph (R1100R), 117 mph (R1100GS), 115 mph (R1150GS), 125 mph (R1100RT), 139 mph (R1100S)

No performance figures available for R850R

Oilheads tend to exhibit a lean surge at part-throttle operation; there are fixes out there that help, but it is a characteristic of the bike.

R259s tend to eat more clutches than airhead models; unfortunately they are also more difficult and costly to replace.

As in the last chapter, expect to replace the Paralever rear bearing on high-mileage bikes.

When the ABS performs its start-up self-check, it sounds like someone trying to start a mistimed John Deere 410 backhoe on ether. Ignore the distinctly agricultural sounds—it's normal.

If the ABS light stays on after start-up, it means that the system is not functioning. The bike can still be ridden normally, but ABS malfunctions can be extremely expensive to repair.

R1200C
(1997-2003)

Chapter 16
BMW's Easy Rider

It had to happen—the Cruiser market was just too big a piece of pie for BMW to pass by. True to form, though, BMW did more than tart up an existing bike. Visually, the 1200C was a knockout. The bike was awash in a sea of chrome and polish. Rather than disguise the Telelever mounts as the other bikes do, the C incorporates them into the design. The upper mount is an attractive aluminum casting that also hides the oil coolers. The rear subframe is constructed of steel tubing painted to look like aluminum. Because the Paralever would have looked too "tech," the C uses an alteration of the Monolever-type swing arm.

Engine modifications are singular to the C. For starters, a larger bore and lengthened stroke boosted displacement to 1,170 cc. The valves, both intake and exhaust, are smaller than those in the other R259 engines, and the camshafts have less lift and overlap. Horsepower, at 61, is the lowest of any of the oilheads—but with 72 ft-lb of torque on hand at 3,000 rpm, who needs horsepower? Other features included waterproof leather grips and bucket seat, and a neat rider's backrest that doubles as a passenger pad—although you have to be very good friends with the passenger. If a custom ride is your thing and you like to shine chrome, the R1200C might be just the ticket.

What They Said at the Time

"Most manufactures try to go in the same direction as Harley-Davidson, but BMW doesn't follow anybody. The R1200 has its own character. I think it's really good. It's not like most Japanese cruisers. Most Japanese cruisers have the same feeling as everybody else's. This is unique. It's an American-style cruiser, but with BMW's thinking. That's good, I like it."
Akihiko Hikida, GK Design, Lakewood, California

BMW Buyer's Guide Spec Sheet— Customs R1200C (1997-2003)

Engine type ——————— Overhead valve, air/oil cooled, flat twin, 4 valve, cam-in-head design
Displacement ————— 1170 cc
Compression ratio ——— 10.0:1
Ignition ————————— Bosch electronic
Carburetion ————————— EFI
Horsepower ——————— 61 bhp @ 5,000 rpm
Electrical System ——— 12 volt, alternator
Transmission ————————— 5-speed, shaft driven
Weight ——————————— 482 lbs
Instruments —————————— Speedometer, warning lights for neutral, high-beam, low oil pressure, low fuel, ABS malfunction
Frame —————————————— Cast aluminum front section, tubular steel rear
Suspension —————————— Telelever front, Monolever rear
Tire size ——————————— 100/90 × 18 front, 170/80 × 18 rear
0-60 ——————————————— Slow
Standing start 1/4 mile — Really slow
Top speed ——————————— 104 mph

No serious or chronic problems have cropped up yet on any of the C models.

Because the engine has grown, so has the vibration; expect a slightly higher vibration level on the C than on other oilheads.

F650, F650GS (1997)

Chapter 17
The Single Life

BMW needed some sort of entry-level bike, something to entice a new rider, or women perhaps. Preferably something with a catchy name. What they got was what might seem to be a lightly warmed over Rotax-powered Aprilia Pegaso with a silly name, the "Funduro." But don't let anyone kid you. There are substantial differences between the Aprilia engine and the one fitted to the F650. Although both are liquid-cooled engines, produced and initially designed by the Austrian firm Rotax, BMW did some serious reengineering before putting their name on the tank. The 48-horsepower BMW version uses a four-valve head and plain bearings, compared to the Rotax-designed version with its five valves and roller bearings. The BMW engine also breathes through dual 33-millimeter Mikuni carburetors, compared to the Aprilia's one.

Power is transmitted via five-speed transmission, and a chain final drive, the first in BMW's history. A conventional single-shock rear swing arm is fitted, as is a conventional telescopic front fork. The F650ST or Strada, a pure street model, uses an 18-inch front wheel and 17-inch rear. The F650 Funduro, a semidual sport version, employs a 19-inch front wheel.

The steel frame was made in Italy, and its upper section contains the dry-sump engine's oil reservoir. A 4.6-gallon plastic tank blends nicely into the enduro-style fairing. (Later versions would have the tank relocated under the seat.) Standard equipment includes a luggage rack and skid plate.

For vertically challenged riders, a lowering kit is available to drop the overall height of the bike by 2 inches.

During the first few years of production, the "baby BMWs" were assembled by Aprilia in Italy, under BMW's direct supervision. After the 2000 model year, production was shifted back to Germany, and the bikes given another redesign. The new F models are now fuel-injected, belt-driven, and expensive.

What They Said at the Time

"Holy mackerel, isn't $7,900 a little steep for an entry level bike?" Unnamed journalist at the U.S. press intro of the F650

BMW Buyer's Guide Spec
Late singles, F650, F650GS (1993-2000)
(Aprillia-built versions)

Engine type ————————— DOHC, liquid cooled, 4-valve single
Displacement ———————— 652 cc
Compression ratio ————— 10.0:1
Ignition ————————————— CDI
Carburetion ———————————— Dual 33mm Mikuni Carburetors
Horsepower ————————————— 48 bhp @ 6,500 rpm
Electrical system ——————— 12 volt, alternator
Transmission ——————————— 5-speed, chain driven (latest models use belts)
Weight ——————————————— 416 lbs
Instruments ———————————— Speedometer, tachometer, warning lights for high-beam, turn signals, neutral
Frame ————————————————— Single downtube, welded steel cradle
Suspension ————————————— Telescopic front fork, swing arm rear
Tire size —————————————— 100/90 × 19 front, 130/80 × 17 rear (Funduro); 100/90 × 18 front, 130/80 × 17 rear (standard model)
0-60 —————————————————— n/a
Standing start 1/4 mile — 13.64 seconds
Top speed ——————————— 101 mph

Late-model bikes, built after 2000, have some fuel injection glitches; they are also heavy, slow, and even more expensive. Of them all, the limited production Dakar version is the most interesting.

Unfortunately the new singles have much in common with the old singles—that is, they are heavy, slow, and expensive.

F650s, being primarily entry-level bikes, get used and abused. Look for worn chains and sprockets, cracked and chipped bodywork and other signs of new riderism.

K75s
(1985-1996)

Chapter 18

Three's Never a Crowd

Ostensibly, the three-cylinder K bike was created by simply loping off one cylinder of a K100, creating a "Flying Brick-et" so to speak. Introduced in 1985, the 3/4-liter triple managed to remain in production until 1996, a respectable run by any standard. During that time, four versions were produced, all with the same basic running gear. All K75s used an identical liquid-cooled, fuel-injected, double overhead cam 750-cc power plant. The engine utilized a counterbalancer to reduce vibration, making the bike turbine smooth. As with the rest of the K line, the engine is positioned in a "lay down" configuration, that is with the cylinder head on the left-hand side of the frame, the crankshaft positioned on the right and the sump in the center. The two-valve-per-cylinder 70-horsepower mill was endowed with a large, easy-to-use torque curve, making the model a favorite with riders who prized a smooth, easy-to-ride motorcycle over some of the more "exciting" bikes available at the time.

The chassis was built from mild steel tubing, using a bridge configuration, the engine and five-speed transmission acting as a stressed member. The swing arm uses the Monolever configuration, while the front fork is a more or less conventional telescopic design. (More on that later.) All models have twin disc brakes at the front and a single disc at the rear, with the exception of the C, which makes do with both a drum brake and 18-inch rear wheel. The rest of the line-up uses the 17-inch rear wheel, as fitted to the K100.

During its career, the K75 earned a reputation as a "thinking man's" motorcycle. It was never the fastest nor best handling bike in the world. But it was smooth, quick, and nimble, the type of machine you could ride for hours on end. Like most BMWs, it was also dead reliable and with some exceptions very easy to repair if something did go sour.

K75C 1985–1988

This was the first iteration of the 750 triple. The bike looked quite the business: a small café type fairing, reminiscent of the R90S was fitted, as were flat bars. There was also a cut down seat option, which made the bike more attractive to those of smaller statute. This was the only model to use the 18-inch rear wheel and drum brake.

K75 (T) 1986–1995

The T was the standard, upright seating model. If the phrase had been in use at the time this would have been the "standard" or "retro" version. The fairing was dropped and the bars were raised. The 17-inch rear wheel and attendant disc brake replaced the old drum brake setup. This was a good all-around motorcycle, very easy to live with, and comfortable with a nice light feel to it. It wasn't considered very fast even then, but a look at the spec sheet shows a 122-mile per hour top end, and a 13.24 quarter-mile at 100.55 miles per hour, which is fast enough to lose your license in any state that I can think of.

K75S 1986–1995

I would have guessed that this was the most popular of the K75 series. It wasn't—that honor goes the RT version by a mere 215 units: 18,878 (RT) to 18,663 (S). To the base K75 package, the S added a three-quarter fairing and chin spoiler. RS-type flat bars were installed to tuck the rider in. The big news was the new front fork. Unlike any other street bike fork at the time, BMW chose to install all of the damping in the left fork leg. Both fork legs had springs installed, but the right leg had only oil—no damping of any sort was used. The new fork greatly reduced front-end dive under hard braking and gave the bike a nice, taut feel. The rear shock was also upgraded with a stiffer spring. Unfortunately, the stiffer spring often overpowered the rebound damping of the rear shock, allowing it to top out a little too freely. Don't be surprised to see some sort of aftermarket rear shock fitted in its place. The K75S is another easy BMW to like. When the optional bags were fitted, the bike became a very competent high-speed sport tourer. During the work week, it could be pressed into yeoman duty, carrying you back and forth to the job. On Sunday, it could hammer racer road with the best of them, particularly if the road had lots of fast sweeping turns.

K75RT 1990–1995

Slap the K100RT's barn door fairing onto a K75 and badda-bing, badda-boom, you've got yourself a full-dress tourer. Albeit not quite so top shelf as the K100RT, it was a whole lot cheaper. Because of that, it quickly found a home among European constabulary. The Euro-cops liked the bike because it was fast enough to run down most of the Euro-trash and comfortable enough to do it day in and day out. In the United States, riders—notably solo riders who liked all the amenities but didn't need or particularly want the four-cylinder version or its price tag—gravitated toward the K75RT. In fact a nicely optioned out RT could often be had for somewhat less than a base model K100RT, making this a very attractive model to the enthusiast with champagne tastes and a beer budget.

What They Said at the Time

"Certainly the author regards the ride from the Arctic Circle to Gibraltar as being one of the most enjoyable of his motorcycling career." Bruce Preston, *BMW Motorcycles: The Complete Story*, commenting on his 10-day, 3,700-mile test ride of the K75C

"[K75 is] "It's a bike of subtle joys." *Cycle World*, May 1993

K75S: "For those riders seeking a complete sport-touring package, capable of devouring days of adventure-filled miles, the K75S is a terrific motorcycle." *Cycle World*, July 1991

"I like it. It's more comfortable than my old S and I don't push it that hard, but I can cruise along all day at 80—besides it was cheaper than a K100." K75RT owner, who prefers to remain nameless, Marcus Dairy (popular Sunday gathering spot for motorcyclists in Connecticut), Summer 2000.

BMW Buyer's Guide Spec Sheet— K75 All (1985–1995)

Engine type	DOHC, water cooled, 2-valves-per-cylinder in-line triple
Displacement	740 cc
Compression ratio	10.5:1
Ignition	Bosch electronic
Carburetion	Bosch Jetronic fuel injection, three 34mm throttle bodies
Horsepower	75 bhp @ 8,500 rpm
Electrical system	12 volt, alternator
Transmission	5-speed, shaft driven
Weight	502 lbs
Instruments	Speedometer, tachometer, digital clock, warning lights for low oil pressure, alternator, choke on, brake, tail light check, fuel level, indicators for high-beam, turn signal, and neutral
Frame	Double downtube, welded steel
Suspension	Telescopic front fork, Monolever rear swing arm
Tire size	100/90 × 18 front, 120/90 × 18 rear
0-60	4.2 seconds
Standing start 1/4 mile	13.3 seconds (K75C)
Top speed	121 mph (K75C)

ABS light may flash when the battery voltage drops, even though there is enough current left to start the bike. While this is sometimes a problem with any of the ABS-equipped models, the K75 seems the most sensitive.

ABS-equipped K75s seem to have a higher than normal incidence of ABS control unit failures.

Dry driveshaft splines occasionally cause lurching and overly sensitive clutch action.

K Bikes (1983-2003)

Chapter 19
Flying Bricks

To the true believer it was sacrilege, a violation of doctrine so severe that it was heretical. Real BMW motorcycles were to have two cylinders, and two cylinders only, and they were to be positioned transversely. In extreme circumstances they could have one cylinder, but those bikes had to have been built before 1966. Any deviation was verboten!

Good thing no one at BMW took the howling mobs too seriously. Rumor had it that a new BMW was in the pipeline. The scuttlebutt was that the new bike was big, fast and had more than two cylinders. The rumors were pretty accurate, for in October 1983, almost 60 years to the day after BMW had debuted the R32, the motorcycling public caught its first glimpse of the "new" BMW—lo and behold! It was big, it was fast, and it had four cylinders.

The boxer faithful were stunned, and frankly, not that many of them were particularly happy. That would change after the initial shock wore off—approximately half of the new K owners would come from the twin-cylinder ranks.

Had the early Honda Gold Wing not used a flat-four layout, the K series might have been called a "flying pancake." Since the last thing BMW managers wanted was a copy of a Honda languishing on the showroom floor, they decided to use an inline four. BMW had extensive experience with the inline arrangement in its car line.

The basic engine platform is a four-cylinder, liquid-cooled, DOHC design. Depending on the year and model, either two or four valve heads are used, and displacement varies from 1,000 to 1,200 cc. The cylinder bores are plated and cast in-unit with the block. The engine is installed in a lay-down configuration—

that is, the head is on the left side of the frame, the crank on the right side, and the bolted-on sump hangs beneath. Because the crankshaft isn't positioned in the center of the frame, a secondary shaft mounted below the crankshaft and driven via spur gears is used to transmit power to the single-plate dry clutch. A five-speed transmission bolts to the back of the engine.

Introductory models employed Bosch LE Jetronic fuel injection and Bosch digital ignition. Over the years these were superseded by Bosch Motronic systems. Valves are adjusted via shims. Frankly, the K bike's engine isn't anything that the shade tree mechanic will find user-friendly.

The engine and transmission are suspended from a light, fairly stiff tube frame. The rear swing arm was initially a Monolever-type setup, although the later bikes used the Paralever design. Initially, standard forks were fitted; in the late 1990s these were exchanged for a modified Telelever.

In an effort to keep the wheelbase down to some sort of manageable proportions, the swing arm fastened directly to the transmission, making the whole engine/transmission and swing arm a tidy, compact unit, which BMW was quick to christen "the compact drive system."

The K100 was equipped with an 18-inch front wheel, sporting dual disc brakes and a 17-inch rear wheel, with a single disc brake. ABS was first offered as an option, starting with the 1987 bikes, although so many of the K bikes were ordered with it that it may as well have been standard.

Overall, the K series had that typical Teutonic futuristic styling that people like Fritz Lang seemed to find so fascinating back in the 1920s. Nonetheless, the faired-in headlight and shrouded fuel tank/radiator were attractive, and the bike was an instant success, much to the dismay of true two cylinder aficionados. In later years, the K series in general has become a much sought-after motorcycle, markedly among those who like to rack up lots and lots of miles in complete comfort.

K100 (1983–1989)

The standard version, the K100 was released to the U.S. market in 1984, to be sold as a 1985 model bike. It received an enthusiastic reception despite being cited by the motorcycling press for a few minor flaws. Complaints centered on three issues, all of which were resolved down the line. Foremost was vibration: like most inline fours, the K100 tended to be a bit buzzy, notably at higher rpm. Smoking on start-up was also a problem. Oil tended to sneak past the ring end-gaps when the bike was parked—leaving it on the kickstand exacerbated the situation. Initially, owners were cautioned to park the bike only on the centerstand. Lastly, there was some static over the torque reaction of the big four. Whenever the throttle was "blipped," particularly when the bike was at a stop, the rotational force of the crankshaft tried to turn the bike to the right. Since this was only a problem when the bike was at a standstill, it was largely ignored.

The naked K bike was the perfect platform for the roll-your-own crowd, who festooned it with everything from touring windshields and bucket seats to turbo chargers. Finding a bone stock K100 may be difficult these days, as most have seen some sort of modification. On the other side of the coin, the naked K100 was only sold in the United States during 1985 and 1986, making finding one at all problematic.

K100RS, TWO-VALVE (1983–1989)

The 100RS was the flagship of the line. It was fast, swoopy, and the best handling BMW to come down the pike in a long time. It was voted Motorcycle of the Year in five European countries, the United States, and Japan. Obvious differences between it and the standard K included a full sport fairing and low bars. Other than that, the running gear is the same. The cockpit includes full instrumentation, including a warning light that won't go off until the engine is running and both brake levers depressed. The fairing incorporates breakaway signals and a wind deflector. Post-1987 bikes may have optional ABS brakes—whether this is a good thing or not is up to you.

K100RS FOUR-VALVE (1990–1992)

Released as a 1991 model, the four-valve version of the RS was much improved compared to its predecessors. In fact, in every measurable way it was considered a better bike than the K1 superbike, the platform that donated most of the good bits. The engine's four-valve head was the big news. By using four small valves and downsizing the ports to match, the new engine managed to make at least 85 percent of its peak torque available between 3,000 rpm and redline. In the real world this meant that the bike would start to pull smoothly from 1,500 rpm and keep making power right up to the 8,500-rpm redline. The engine management package was a Bosch Motronic ignition/fuel injection unit that employed 3-D mapping. Compared to the K1, the four-valve used a slightly lowered rear end ratio; this gave it some advantage in acceleration in the 45 to 75-mile per hour range, the range where most big road burners spend most of their time. The old Monolever swing arm was replaced with a Paralever, a much-appreciated change.

Some of the other suspension "upgrades" weren't so well received. The rear shock was lifted straight from the K75S, and it was just too soft. Likewise, the front fork spring was a tad light, and heavy braking could drop the RS fork right onto the fork stops. ABS was a listed option. Overall, the bike garnered high marks from everyone who tried it. Complaints were few, and they revolved primarily around the soft suspension, a matter easily put right with aftermarket parts.

K1 (1989–1993)

Like Stymie used to say, "Re-mark-able." At some point I suppose they just decided that enough was enough and it was time to build a super bike. First the engine was tricked out with a four-valve head, the double overhead cams acting directly against bucket-style tappets. No shims are used to adjust clearances; if the valves need adjusting, a thicker or thinner bucket is required. The good news is that the recommended adjustment interval is every 18,000 miles. The compression was raised from the two-valve engine's 10.2:1 to a slightly stiffer 11:1. The new piston also got a revised oil control ring to prevent oil from draining into the combustion chamber whenever the bike was parked on the kickstand. In the bottom end, the crankshaft lost almost three pounds. This allowed the engine to rev quicker. On the induction side, the old swinging door air meter and Jetronic fuel management system was dumped for an up-to-date Motronic air density system that greatly increased air flow—a requirement brought on by the new, deep breathing head. A short muffler connected to an expansion chamber under the five-speed gearbox underscored the sporting intentions of the new engine. To make better use of the new engine's power, the rear end ratio was revised to a slightly taller 2.75:1, as compared to the standard model's 2.81:1.

To house the revised mill, a new frame was created. The front down tubes grew in diameter from 30 to 32 millimeters, while the rear seat tubes gained an extra 13 millimeters of diameter. In an attempt to add a bit of nimbleness to the admittedly large K1, the rake was reduced to 26.5 degrees and trail reduced to 3.54 inches. (Standard K100 measurements were 27.5 degrees and 4.0 inches, respectively.)

The bike weighed in at a hefty 611 pounds, ready to ride, so 3 inches was added to the handlebars to provide a bit more leverage. The bars were bolted to a 42-millimeter Marzocchi fork. The fork was nonadjustable but provided

5.3 inches of travel. In the rear, a single gas-charged Bilstein shock was bolted to a Paralever-type swing arm, the first time one was used on a K bike. All told, with the new swing arm, the wheelbase of the K1 was a station-wagon-like 61.6 inches.

The new bike rolled on Italian-made FPS wheels, wide for the time at 3.50 inches in front and 4.50 out back. The diameters were reversed compared to the other K bikes—this time the 17-inch was in the front while an 18-inch brought up the rear.

The front brakes were all new and up-to-the-moment four-piston Brembos, with differential pistons designed to equalize pad wear. The floating front rotors were large for the day, 305 millimeters. U.S. models had ABS as standard equipment.

The spec sheet was pretty impressive, but what really got everyone's attention was the seven-piece fairing and tailpiece that enclosed the motorcycle. The front fender was

a two-piece affair that shrouded the front wheel and directed cooling air onto the front brake. The fairing was strikingly finished in deep red or blue, set off with K1 graphics and yellow trim. From 1991 on, the styling was toned down a bit. While the K1 was a real head turner and quite the business, it never sold particularly well. The plain fact was that the four-valve K100RS performed better and was cheaper.

K100RT (1984–1989)

Fancy a go at the Iron Butt do you? The K100RT might be just the ticket. Built along the same lines as the base K100, the RT featured an upright seating position and barn door fairing. At the risk of giving a good motorcycle the bum's rush, I can only say the K RT is a just like all of the RTs that came before it, only there is more of it.

K100LT (1986–1991)

If the K100RT was the plain vanilla touring bike, the LT was the hot fudge sundae with nuts and an extra cherry. As you may guess, the LT stood for luxury touring, and that's what you got. On top of the standard RT package, expect to find a blacked out engine, anatomically correct and extremely comfortable saddle, a tail trunk, factory-installed radio mounting kit (the radio was a $495 option), a theft alarm, two accessory outlets, a four-way emergency flasher, extended rear fender mud-flap, and a black crash bar. Lastly, origi-

...nent included a self-leveling Boge-Nivomat shock ...hich was an option on the rest of the K line.

K1100RS (1993–1996)

... K11, using almost square engine dimen-... millimeters (bore and stroke) now dis-placed 1,092 cc. The fairing had grown more angular and in many ways even more attractive, and the Paralever controlled rear end antics. Showa supplied both the front and rear suspension. The chassis geometry was revised once again; rake was now 26 degrees, and trail 3.7 inches. A limited RSL version was also available with both ABSII and more complete instrumentation.

K1200RS (1997–2003)

This is the mack daddy of all K bikes. Released in 1997, the K1200RS starts with an honest 130 horsepower mill, rubber-mounted in a cast-aluminum frame that eliminates any trace of vibration. The front suspension is now a revised version of the Telelever—the lever arm bolting to the frame, rather than the engine as it does on the R models. Likewise, the Paralever shock is mounted to the frame. The K12 features the third generation of the Bosch Motronic engine management package. Advantages? No choke lever, and a mobile diagnostic computer, the Bosch "Mobi-Dic," can be used to troubleshoot problems. The transmission was upgraded to a six-speed and 17-inch wheels fitted, with radial tires. ABS comes standard. A slick new fairing, wind tunnel developed, features a two-way adjustable windshield.

K1200LT (1999–2003)

I saved this one for last, simply because it is quite easily one of the most impressive bikes I've ever ridden. The basic engine architecture is similar to that of the RS version although revised somewhat to meet touring duties. As with the RS, the frame is aluminum, and both a Telelever and Paralever handle suspension duties. The wheelbase is a lengthy 64.2 inches, which BMW claims is required to provide the room and ride that the average LT customer wants. The bodywork is fully integrated with nonremovable saddle bags and top trunk. The cockpit area is sealed to prevent drafts from reaching the rider and passenger. The fairing and windshield provide unheard of weather protection, and the windshield is adjustable at the touch of a button, with a 5-inch range. The radio is standard on the K1200LT, and comes with four speakers and separate controls for the rider and passenger. To ease parking chores, an electric reverse is installed in the 5-speed gearbox. Cruise control is a standard feature, as is ABS. For those year-round riders, heated grips, optional on most of the other bikes, are standard on the K1200LT.

Three versions of the bike are available: the LT, the LT-I (Icon), which adds a trip-computer and CD changer, and the LT-C (custom), which adds all of the above plus extra chrome and specially contoured heated seat and backrest. The bike is fast, it handles like a dream, and it is easily the most comfortable long-distance bike I've ever been on; beside it's the only motorcycle I can think of that lists a refrigerator as an option. Expect to pay top dollar for one of these, if you can even find one.

What They Said at the Time

"Europe's most important new bike in a generation." Preview of the K100, *Cycle*, January 1984

"The K100RS is a bike that can be herded along a twisty ribbon of road in the company of the best high-performance Japanese iron without losing its stately composure." *Cycle World*, September 1984

"The new model [K100RS, four-valve] advances BMW's state of the art in performance; for that the faithful can rejoice in the bike's exclusivity and push their average speeds up a few more miles per hour." *Cycle*, April 1991

"The K1 represents the only all-European, multicylinder answer to the Japanese superbikes." *Cycle*, August 1989

"You've heard of das boot? Here's das full boot." "Germany has finally delivered." Comments on the K100LT, *Cycle*, July 1987

"With the K1100RS you do get a lot for your money. You get a machine that can run head to head with the best in the class." *Cycle World*, June 1993

"The K1200RS is a very good bike, a mile eater-par excellence that won't be disgraced along racer road." *Cycle World*, July 1997

"This new and biggest BMW has Honda's sybaritic Gold Wing dancing in the cross hairs." Preview of the K1200LT, *Cycle World*, December 1998

BMW Buyer's Guide Spec Sheet—
K100, K1100, K1200, K1, 4-valve (1983–2000)
K100 (All versions RS, RT, LT 1983–1989)

Engine type —————— DOHC, liquid cooled, 2-valves-per-cylinder inline 4
Displacement ——————— 987 cc
Compression ratio ————— 10.2:1
Ignition —————————— Bosch electronic
Carburetion ——————— Bosch fuel injection
Horsepower —————————— 90 bhp @ 8,000 rpm (all 1,000cc, two-valve engines)
Electrical system ———————— 12 volt alternator
Transmission —————————— 5-speed, shaft driven
Weight —————————— 527 lbs (K100), 558 lbs (K100RS), 580 lbs (K100RT)
Instruments ———————— Speedometer, tachometer, digital clock, warning lights for low oil pressure, alternator, choke on, brake, tail light check, fuel level, indicators for high-beam, turn signal, and neutral
Frame —————————— Double downtube, welded steel
Suspension ——————————— Telescopic front fork, Monolever rear swing arm
Tire size ——————————— 100/90 × 18 front, 130/90 × 17 rear
0-60 ——————————————— 3.9 seconds (K100RS), 3.92 seconds (K100LT)
Standing start 1/4 mile — 12.56 seconds (K100RS), 12.86 seconds (K100LT)
Top speed ————————————— 122 mph (measured, K100RS), n/a (K100LT)

BMW Buyer's Guide Spec Sheet—
K100, 4-valve (1990–1992)

Engine type —————— DOHC, liquid cooled, 4-valves-per-cylinder inline four
Displacement ——————— 987 cc
Compression ratio ————— 11.2:1
Ignition —————————— Bosch electronic
Carburetion ——————— Bosch Motronic fuel injection, four 35mm throttle bodies
Horsepower ——————————— 100 bhp @ 7,500 rpm
Electrical system ———————— 12 volt, alternator
Transmission ————————— 5-speed, shaft driven
Weight —————————— 639 lbs
Instruments ———————— Speedometer, tachometer, digital clock, warning lights for low oil pressure, alternator, choke on, brake, tail light check, fuel level, indicators for high-beam, turn signal, neutral, and ABS malfunction warning
Frame —————————— Double downtube, welded steel
Suspension ——————————— Telescopic front fork, Paralever rear swing arm
Tire size ——————————— 120/70 × 17 front, 160/60 × 18 rear
0-60 ——————————————— 3.3 seconds
Standing start 1/4 mile — 11.98 seconds
Top speed ————————— 140 mph

BMW Buyer's Guide Spec Sheet—
K1 (1989–1993)

Engine type	DOHC, liquid cooled, 4-valves-per-cylinder inline four
Displacement	987 cc
Compression ratio	11.0:1
Ignition	Bosch electronic
Carburetion	Bosch Motronic fuel injection, four 35mm throttle bodies
Horsepower	100 bhp @ 7,500 rpm (95 bhp on US versions modified to pass EPA emission tests)
Electrical system	12 volt, alternator
Transmission	5-speed, shaft driven
Weight	569 lbs
Instruments	Speedometer, tachometer, digital clock, warning lights for low oil pressure, alternator, choke on, brake, tail light check, fuel level, indicators for high-beam, turn signal, neutral, and ABS malfunction warning
Frame	Double downtube, welded steel
Suspension	Marzocchi telescopic front fork, Paralever rear swing arm
Tire size	120/70 × 17 front, 160/60 × 17 rear
0-60	4.1 seconds
Standing start 1/4 mile	12.08 seconds
Top speed	143 mph

BMW Buyer's Guide Spec Sheet— K1100RS, K1100RT (1992–1996)

Engine type	DOHC, liquid cooled, 4-valves-per-cylinder inline four
Displacement	1,093 cc
Compression ratio	11.0:1
Ignition	Bosch electronic
Carburetion	Bosch Motronic fuel injection
Horsepower	87.2 bhp @ 7,500 rpm (dyno tested at rear wheel)
Electrical system	12 volt, alternator
Transmission	5-speed, shaft driven
Weight	592 lbs (K1100RS), 649 lbs (K1100LT)
Instruments	Speedometer, tachometer, digital clock, warning lights for low oil pressure, alternator, choke on, brake, tail light check, fuel level, indicators for high-beam, turn signal, neutral, and ABS malfunction
Frame	Double downtube, welded steel
Suspension	Marzocchi telescopic front fork, Paralever rear swing arm
Tire size	120/70 × 17 front, 160/60 × 18 rear (K1100RS); 110/80 × 18 front, 140/80 × 17 rear (K1100LT)
0-60	3.4 seconds (K1100RS), 3.5 seconds (K1100RT)
Standing start 1/4 mile	11.71 seconds (K1100RS), 12.12 seconds (K1100LT)
Top speed	139 mph (K1100RS), 125 mph (K1100LT)

BMW Buyer's Guide Spec Sheet— K1200RS, K1200LT (1999–2003)

Engine type	DOHC, liquid cooled, 4-valves-per-cylinder inline four
Displacement	1,171 cc
Compression ratio	11.5:1 (K1200RS), 10.8:1 (K1200LT)
Ignition	Bosch electronic
Carburetion	Bosch Motronic fuel injection, four 38mm throttle bodies (K1200RS), four 34mm throttle bodies (K1200LT)
Horsepower	130 bhp @ 7,500 rpm (K1200RS), 98 bhp @ 7,500 rpm (K1200LT)
Electrical system	12 volt, alternator
Transmission	6-speed, shaft driven, K1200LT equipped with reverse
Weight	613 lbs (K1200RS), 834 lbs (K1200LT)
Instruments	Speedometer, tachometer, digital clock, warning lights for low oil pressure, alternator, choke on, brake, tail light check, fuel level, indicators for high-beam, turn signal, neutral, and ABS malfunction
Frame	Aluminum
Suspension	Telelever front fork, Paralever rear swing arm
Tire size	120/70 × 17 front, 170/60 × 17 rear
0-60	3.3 seconds (K1200RS), n/a (K1200LT)
Standing start 1/4 mile	11.28 seconds (K1200RS), 13.83 seconds (K1200LT)
Top speed	150 mph (K1200RS)

Early bikes tend to smoke quite a bit on start-up, particularly if parked on the kickstand. Bikes built after 1989 with pinned piston rings and a modified breather system are much better.

Early K models tended to strip the damper hub on the secondary shaft, essentially preventing forward motion of the motorcycle and requiring a complete engine teardown to resolve the problem.

Heat coming off the engine, past the radiator and up from the exhaust wears out some riders. The situation is worst on the early bikes, improves through the 1100 series and is minimal on the 1200s.

Occasionally the fuel pump, located inside the tank, can get a bit noisy. This seems to affect individual bikes regardless of year more than a particular model run.

Early Motronic injection systems as installed on the K1 and four-valve models have one drawback: because the system uses a preprogrammed map, engine, or exhaust modifications may confuse it. If you're looking at a modified bike that uses a Motronic system, make certain there are no hidden glitches that the seller has been unable to "tune" out.

Vibration has always been an issue with K bikes; as with most everything, the early K bikes were most afflicted, and later bikes much improved.

One of the things that make BMW ownership fun is the tight knit community of enthusiasts. This includes parts suppliers, clubs, and the dealer network. These guys always seem willing to lend a helping hand, supply you with parts, or provide a shoulder to cry on. The folks listed here are people I've personally dealt with or who've been recommended by folks I trust. It's by no means complete, and any omission is simply the result of time and space constraints.

PARTS SUPPLIERS

Accessory Mart (DomiRacer)
P.O. Box 26116
Cincinnati, Ohio 45226
(513) 871-1678
These guys have nearly everything you can think of, including bikes. A great source for anything made in Europe or the U.K.

Blue Moon Cycle
752 W. Peachtree Street
Norcross, GA 30071
(770) 447-6945
If it's BMW and old, give these guys a call.

Bing Agency International
P.O. Box 1, 101 South Main
Belvedere, KS 67028
(316) 862-5808
The name says it all; one stop shopping for Bing carburetors and parts.

BMW Motorrad St. Louis/Sidecar Restorations
4011 Forest Park Blvd.
St. Louis, MO 63108
Everything BMW, especially if it's sidecar related.

Bob's BMW
10630 Riggs Hill Road
Jessup, MD 20794
(888) 269-2627
New, used, or remanufactured, get it at Bob's.

Capitol Cycle
45449 Severn Way, Suite 179
Sterling, VA, 21066-8918
(800) 642-5100
In the business since 1971, Capitol claims to be the largest supplier of /2 parts in North America. I don't doubt it. They can supply most parts from 1955 on up.

CLUBS

BMW Motorcycle Owners of America
P.O. Box 489
Chesterfield, MO 63006-0489
Probably the biggest club; lots of rallies and a great magazine with good technical information.

BMW Riders' Association
P.O. Box 510309
Melbourne Beach, FL 32951
Not so big, but very enthusiastic.

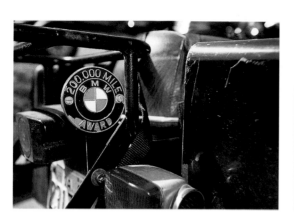

Bob's BMW

Vintage BMW Motorcycle Owners, Ltd.
P.O. Box 67
Exeter, NH 03833
You guessed it, devoted to the oldies.

PRINTED MATTER
Books
I'd recommend the following to anyone who's the least bit enthusiastic about BMW motorcycles.

BMW Motorcycles
Darwin Holmstrom and Brian J. Nelson
(MBI) ISBN 0-7603-1098-x

Illustrated Buyer's Guide BMW Motorcycle
Knittel & Slabon,
(MBI) ISBN 0-7603-0082-8

BMW Motorcycles—The Complete Story
Bruce Preston
(Crowood Press Ltd.)
ISBN 1-86-126-005-9

BMW Twins—The Complete Story
Mick Walker
(Crowood Press Ltd.)
ISBN 1-86126-153-5

BAHNSTROMER—The Story of BMW Motorcycles
(L.J.K. SetrightTransport Bookman Publications Ltd.)
ISBN 0 85184 021 3

BMW R100RS
Bill Stermer
(Whitehorse Press)
ISBN 1-884313-31-0

Magazines and Road Test Reprints
Walneck's Classic Cycle Trader
P.O. Box 9059
Clearwater, FL 34168
(800) 877-6141
Old road tests, lots and lots of want ads, and an advice column by yours truly.

Hemming's Motor News
P.O. Box 100
Bennington, VT 05201
(800) 277-4373
Hemming's caters to the old car crowd, but they have a growing and informative motorcycle section.

Motorcycle Days
P.O. Box 9686
Baltimore, MD 21237
(410) 665-6295
Magazines, posters, old brochures and who knows what else. If it's on paper and has some thing to do with motorcycles, you can find it here.
Ian Smith Information—Motorcycle Reports
P.O. Box 9440
Denver, CO 80209-0440
(303) 777-2385

Appendix 1

What does it cost to own a BMW? This list represents the average prices of commonly replaced parts, accessories and tools (prices were current at the time this was written). It is intended to be representative and is obviously not a complete listing of all available parts.

Shop Manuals & Parts books

Parts Books
01-09-9-099-161 All 1955–1969s $58.95
01-01-9-796-621 All 1000cc Boxers,
  (1977–1984)   *$74.50
01-01-9-796-611 All R80s,
  (1977–1984)   *$51.45
*(From 1985 to 1997 BMW parts
  books were only available on microfiche)

Shop Manuals
01-59-9-099-176 Earles fork twins $89.50
01-57-9-798-461 All /7 Boxers
  (1977–1984) $74.50
01-57-9-798-797 K75/K100 $108.95

Oil filters
11-42-1-460-845 Spin on filter,
  K & R1100 $11.50
11-42-1-337-572 Oil filter 1970
  and later $7.50
11-42-1-337-575 Hinged, for use
  with oil cooler $12.20

Air filters
13-72-1-341-528 R100, round filter $14.10
13-72-1-460-337 K bike $22.95
13-72-1-250-388 1955–1969
  (non-choke) $22.95

Engine parts
Gasket sets—these contain all gaskets
  needed for a complete engine
  overhaul 11-00-1-460-981 K100 $203.79
11-00-1-255-023 /5/6 through 1975
    $103.95
11-00-9-090-267 R50–R60/2 $102.91

Valve cover gaskets
11-12-1-460-464 K100 inner gasket $4.11
11-12-1-460-463 K100 outer gasket $4.99
11-12-1-338-426 All except R69–R69/S $4.95

Piston Rings
11-25-1-460-994 K100–K75 through
  1/88 $40.51 per set
  (A set is for one piston, so a
  K100 requires four sets)
11-25-1-337-399 R100,
  1981 and later $33.54

Top end rebuild kits (Capitol Cycle, everything needed to overhaul BMW twin cylinder heads except valve seats)
Kit #5 R60/5/6/7 $240.19
Kits run from #5 to # 11 to cover all models

Hardened valve seats for unleaded conversions run from $8.00 to $22.00

Electrics
Point sets
12-11-1-243-555 all models 1970–1978 $7.23
12-11-8-004-116 all models 1955–1969
    $17.42

Diode boards
12-31-244-062 1970 and later $100.83

Carburetor rebuild kits
13-11-1-258-051 Rebuild kit for
  32mm Vacuum Carburetors $49.70
13-11-0-000-Z R50/1 69S rebuild kit $5.15

Exhaust
18-12-1-233-210 Left muffler
  1970–1984 Boxer $176.75
18-12-1-451-527 K100 muffler $477.31
18-087/088 R50/R60 (1955–1969
  reproduction, Capitol Cycle) $344.19

Clutch plate
21-21-1-451-721 K100 $108.11
21-21-1-251-803 1970–1980 Boxer $80.03
21-21-0-070-060 1955–1969 Twins $150.80

Gearbox
Gasket and seal kits
23-00-1-451-775 K75/100 $37.39
23-00-1-233-224 5-speed
  through 1980 $34.27
23-00-9-090-284 1955–1969 $51.95

Front forks
Fork springs
31-42-1-232-017 Heavy duty
  1970–1980 & US/2 $17.62
31-42-1-457-904 K75/K100 $17.63

Steering head bearings
07-11-9-985-070 All 1970
  and later $26.99 (each)

31-41-2-000-000-T Earles fork
  tapered bearing set, (Capitol Cycle) $62.35

Rear shocks   (OEM)
33-53-1-450-850 K100/K75 Monoshock
    $273.00
33-53-1-231-498 1970–1984 Heavy duty
    $119.08

Handle bars
32-71-1-237-659 USA 1970–1978 $59.80
32-71-1-233-126 Euro low bar
  R90S, R100S $82.11
  /2 USA bar $82.11

Levers
32-72-1-457-058 Front brake K75/K100
    $33.80
32-72-1-234-848 1976 on twins $35.88

Cables
32-72-1-450-213
  Clutch cable, K100RS, K75/S $15.55
32-73-2-312-155 Clutch
  cable R1100 $20.28

32-73-1-234-857 Brake cable
  1976–1980 (remote master cylinder) $20.28
32-73-1-234-515 Brake cable
  1955–1975 (drum brake) $21.79

13-21-2-072-348 /2 twins
  w/USA bars $9.46 (each)
32-73-2-312-148 R1100 $47.32

Brakes
34-21-1-230-265 Upper rear shoe
  1970–1980 $48.83
34-21-1-230-265 Lower rear shoe
  1970–180 $47.32
34-11-2-301-358 Brake pads
  1974–1980 except R65 $48.36
34-31-1-234-927 Master cylinder
  rebuild kit dual disc, 1976–1980 $46.28

Wheels
36-31-1-234-591 Spokes 18"
  all /2, /5, /6, /7 (40 required) $1.04
36-31-1-450-859 Bearings
  front, 1985 and later $10.92 (each)

36-31-1-451-897 Front cast wheel,
 K75/K1001985 and later, boxer $337.95

Body work
46-61-1-234-931 Primed front fender
 all 1974–1984 except GS, ST, R65 $92.04
46-61-1-450-668 Primed front
 fender K100 $145.60
46-62-1-240-397 Matte black rear
 fender all 1970–1984 $186.68
46-51-4-034-260 Right side foot peg
 1955–1984 $21.32
46-63-1-234-852 Right side battery
 cover matte black 1974 and later $74.57
46-63-1-231-853 Black/chrome /5 $129.95
52-53-1-237-832 /7 seat thru 1978 $703.56

Instrument cluster
62-11-1-459-352 K100RS/RT
 complete cluster $650.99
62-11-1-243-424 R100/7
 complete cluster $702.99
62-12-1-243-457 Speedometer,
 R100S, RS, RT $184.03

Relays
61-31-1-459-224 Flasher, K75–K100 $80.03
61-31-1-358-194 Flasher,
 /6, /7 thru 1980 $35.31
61-32-1-243-049 Headlight relay
 1979 on except R65 $21.32
61-31-1-379-911 K100 fuel
 injection relay $21.79

Appendix 2: Common Service Prices

Like all manufacturers, BMW lists standard times, known as "flat rates," for all of the common repair procedures. The flat rate is only a suggestion, of course, and dealers are free to charge whatever they want for a given job. However the prices listed below, based on a shop rate of $75.00 per hour, should be right in the ball park for most areas of the country. These prices are for labor only and assume there are no complications. Like the parts prices, these jobs are representative rather than inclusive.

Inspection 1/6,000 mile service (minor): R bikes (airhead) $130.00 RT/R/GS/PD $155.00 K75 $125.00 LT $140.00 RS $130.00 K100/KI100/K12 $130.00

Inspection 2/12,000 mile service (major): R Bikes $295.00 RT $310.00 K bikes $285.00 K1/K1100 LT, with valve adjustment $375.00 16 valve, without valve adjustment $275.00 K75RT $275.00 K1200LT with/without valve adjustment $450.00/$560.00

Retorque heads and adjust valves: R bikes (airhead) $75.00 RS/RT $85.00 K75 $75.00 K75RT $85.00 K1/K11 and RS (1990 and later) $190.00

Annual Service

(includes brake fluid change)	R bike (airhead) $190.00 K bike (with coolant change) $230.00 R1100 $185.00
R1100 Service	6000 $175.00 6000 RT $190.00 12000 $275.00 12000 RT $285.00
Oil and filter change	R bikes $45.00 R bikes with oil cooler $74.00 K bikes $45.00
Gearbox oil change	All bikes $20.00
Fork oil change	All bikes $35.00
Rear drive oil change	All bikes $20.00
Swing arm oil change	R bikes $10.00
Lube input shaft splines	R bikes $295.00 RT or any bike with saddle bags $320.00 K bikes $330.00 RS (1990 and later) $350.00 K1/K1100 $395.00
Bleed brakes/change fluid	R bikes $35.00 K bikes (ABS) $35.00 ABS II $50.00
K coolant change	All $35.00 to $70.00
Adjust steering head bearings	R bikes–all $35.00 K bikes $35.00 RS/RT/LT–all $45.00 K1 $45.00
Replace fork springs	R bikes $90.00 RS/RT $110.00 K $99.00 K11 $200.00
Replace fork seals	R bike $110.00 RS/RT $125.00 K $110.00 K1/K11 $130.00
Replace steering head bearings	All telescopic and Earles fork bikes $295.00
Replace pads–clean disc	R bikes $35.00 K bikes $35.00 K1 $50.00
Replace front brake shoes	$50.00
Replace rear pads/shoes	All R bikes except /2 $35.00 Rear pads $20.00 K1/K11 $20.00
Replace rear main seal & O ring	R bikes includes oil pump seal $360.00 K bikes $370.00 RS (1991 and later) $345.00 K1/K11 $380.00
Replace clutch	R bikes $330.00 RT/RS $345.00 K bikes $340.00 RS (1990 and later) $390.00 K1/K11 $405.00 R1100 (oil head) $450.00
Remove and replace top end (machine work extra)	R bikes $295.00 RS/RT $310.00 K bikes $360.00 RT/LT $410.00 K1/K11 $450.00
R bike, replace timing chain	All–3.5 to 4.0 hours $260.00–$295.00

Index

BMW Motorcycles
ISBN 0-7603-1098-X

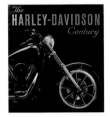

"Harley-Davidson Century"
ISBN: 0760311552

Honda Motorcycles
ISBN: 0-7603-1077-7

**Ducati Desmquattro
Superbikes**
ISBN: 0-7603-1093-9

Triumph Motorcycles
ISBN: 0-7603-0456-4

Ducati Desmoquattro Performance Handbook
ISBN: 0-7603-1236-2

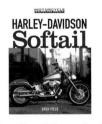

Harley-Davidson Softail
ISBN: 0-7603-1063-7

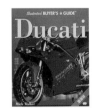

**Ducati Illustrated Buyer's
Guide, 3rd Ed.**
ISBN: 0-7603-1309-1

Original Ducati Supersport
ISBN: 0-7603-0995-7